FORGIVENESS

A Philosophical Study

Joram Graf Haber

Rowman & Littlefield Publishers, Inc.

ROWMAN & LITTLEFIELD PUBLISHERS, INC.

Published in the United States of America
by Rowman & Littlefield Publishers, Inc.
4720 Boston Way, Lanham, Maryland 20706

British Cataloging in Publication Information Available

Library of Congress Cataloging-in-Publication Data

Haber, Joram Graf.
Forgiveness / Joram Graf Haber.
p. cm.
Includes bibliographical references.
1. Forgiveness. I. Title.
BJ1476.H33 1991
179'.9—dc20 91–17869 CIP

ISBN 0–8476–7671–4 (cloth : alk. paper)
ISBN 0–8476–7870–9 (paper : alk. paper)

Printed in the United States of America

™ The paper used in this publication meets the minimum requirements of American National Standard for Information Sciences—Permanence of Paper for Printed Library Materials, ANSI Z39.48–1984.

To My Mother
Zena G. Haber
And to the Memory of My Father
Harry Haber

וַיֹּאמֶר יְהוָה סָלַחְתִּי כִּדְבָרֶךָ

Numbers, XIV:20

Contents

Foreword

I received my basic philosophical education in the late 1940s and early 1950s, and I suspect that my academic experience was matched by almost all other English-speaking students in that period. Although I studied some of the historical classics of moral philosophy, the preoccupations of my teachers and much of my independent reading were set by the concern of Anglo-American writers to analyze the meaning and logical status of so-called ethical statements, "*X* is good" and "*Y* is right" (with the "*X*" and "*Y*" filled in appropriately). While there were some dissenters, these writers tended to distinguish fairly sharply between ethical and meta-ethical inquiries, and they put their own work into the latter category. They assumed that the analysis of the meaning of ethical terms—the answer to such questions as "Is 'good' the name of a property?"—could be pursued in a morally neutral way and many of them maintained that their conclusions held no implications for substantive ethical questions. The great divide between these writers was over the issue of cognitivism *versus* noncognitivism, whether ethical statements could be construed as truth-claims, as assertions of some sort, or rather, as expressions of emotion.

I must confess that I found—and still find—these analytical inquiries to be fascinating and fundamental, but I also thought that a good deal of morality, moral discourse, and the moral life had been left out of consideration. Among many relatively undiscussed topics that might be mentioned was the phenomenon of forgiving, which is the subject of Dr. Joram Haber's book. For all its importance in our everyday morality, I do not recall ever having read any Anglo-American treatment of forgiveness, nor was it ever discussed in a class, and I think I had some excellent courses on ethical theory. I do not think that my student experience was unique, for as recently as 1962 the English philosopher P. F. Strawson could write that forgiveness "is a rather unfashionable subject in moral philosophy. . . ." As Dr. Haber points out, the neglect of such topics as forgiveness stemmed from a more general neglect of the "feeling" side of the moral life.

Undoubtedly, had I read more widely and deeply even in the eighteenth-century British classics of moral philosophy I would have found much to fill up the gaps. Such writers as Butler, Hume, and Smith gave a central place to the moral sentiments in their discussions: guilt, remorse, resentment, shame, pride, and the like. Recent ethical theory has seen a fortunate revival of interest in these and other philosophers who have emphasized that the moral life falls within a general framework of human attitudes and feelings, so that a richer texture has been given to our understanding of many theorists in the tradition, as well as of morality itself; new depths of meaning have been found in Kant, to name just one. Most notable, of course, is the renewed interest in Aristotle and other virtue theorists. As Dr. Haber indicates, moral philosophy is again concerned with what sort of person we should be, and not only with the actions we should perform.

Interest in the topic of forgiveness is concomitant with the above-described trends, and Dr. Haber's book is a significant contribution to the growing literature on it. His treatment deploys the techniques of analytical philosophy. He asks whether "forgiveness" can be defined and whether necessary and sufficient conditions can be supplied for the truth of the statement "I forgive you." His own strategy is to develop a paradigm of the forgiveness situation, a laying out of the standard case of forgiveness, as it were. In line with the speech–act approach developed by the late J. L. Austin, which recognizes that we can do things with words, Dr. Haber treats "I forgive you" as a performative utterance, as a doing of something. On the more normative side, he presents a defense of resentment, arguing that a (morally) injured party's resentment can be connected to his or her self-respect and is therefore justified in various circumstances. Forgiveness, in turn, may be justified, and even called for, when the wrongdoer repents. Against certain writers Dr. Haber argues that forgiveness may be a virtue, that is, when it is permitted by moral principles and not ruled out by other considerations.

Certainly, this is not the place to go into details; for them, the reader is invited to turn to the body of the book. Dr. Haber's analysis of forgiveness is important not only in its own right, but it also opens up areas for further philosophical reflection, for instance, on how forgiveness operates in nonparadigmatic situations; for example, when injury is carelessly but not intentionally inflicted. Joram Haber's book will provide the starting-points for this and other inquiries into a significant feature of our common moral discourse.

Martin P. Golding
Professor of Philosophy and Law
Duke University

Acknowledgments

Like all first books, this one contains both good and bad material. For the bad material, I take sole responsibility. For the good material, I share responsibility with:

Virginia Held, who oversaw the project from start to finish and added valuable comments along the way;

Martin Golding, who took time out from his own important work to give this book his imprimatur;

Jeffrie Murphy and Kathleen Dean Moore, who were available to answer questions I needed answered along the way;

The philosophy faculties at Clark University and C. W. Post College, who were audiences to topics that became parts of this book;

Walter Brand, who provided a sounding board on whom I would test my ideas out;

Pat Merrill, Terre Jacobs-Rieder, and Milton Kornrich, for their adroit technical assistance; and

My wife, Lina, and son, Joshua, who were patient and supportive throughout this project. (May they both forgive me for all that they endured.)

Acknowledgments also go to:

John Langshaw Austin, *How to Do Things with Words* (Cambridge, Mass.: Harvard University Press, 1962). Copyright © 1962 by the President and Fellows of Harvard College; reprinted by permission of the publishers.

H. J. N. Horsbrugh, "Forgiveness," *Canadian Journal of Philosophy*, 4, no. 2 (December 1974). Reprinted by permission of the publishers.

Jeffrie G. Murphy and Jean Hampton, *Forgiveness and Mercy* (New York: Cambridge University Press, 1988). Reprinted by permission of the publishers.

William Neblett, "Forgiveness and Ideals," *Mind*, 83 (April 1974). Reprinted by permission of Oxford University Press.

Introduction

Forgiveness has often been viewed as morally good and indicative of a merciful character. Despite this, its nature as a moral response has largely been ignored by moral philosophers. In 1962, for instance, P. F. Strawson remarked that "forgiveness . . . is a rather unfashionable subject in moral philosophy."[1] Since then, a number of articles have appeared that have brought to life points of philosophical interest. Among these are R. S. Downie's "Forgiveness,"[2] Jeffrie Murphy's "Forgiveness and Resentment,"[3] Elizabeth Beardsley's "Understanding and Forgiveness,"[4] and Martin Golding's "Forgiveness and Regret."[5] But if the articles that have appeared are philosophically interesting, how are they interesting and why has the subject been largely ignored?

One reason forgiveness is interesting is that it is part of a set of concerns centering on the role of feelings in the moral life. Traditionally, moral philosophy has placed great emphasis on such concepts as "right," "wrong," and "duty"—concepts applicable primarily to actions. Even "the good" tends to be treated as something it is our duty to act to produce or as a property of actions themselves. But the idea that there is a duty to have feelings has always been met with skepticism; for duties are generally taken to concern that which can be performed at will, while feelings are regarded as passions—states beyond the control of the will. At the same time, it cannot be denied that feelings play a role in our moral lives. We teach that certain feelings and attitudes ought to be had, such as being grateful for gifts and generous with money.

Over the past fifteen years, there has been increasing interest in the role of feelings as philosophers have returned to the approach of Aristotle—to a study of the virtues with an emphasis not so much on what a moral agent should *do* as on what kind of person a moral agent should *be*. This interest has grown out of a dissatisfaction with the methodological commitment to the primacy of moral principles that has been the hallmark of ethics ever since Kant. Deontologists and consequentialists have tended to de-emphasize a concern with moral "being" in favor of a concentration on moral "doing." These philosophers construe the central question of ethics as asking what we, as responsible moral agents confronting decisions of right and wrong, ought to do. They see it as their task to formulate principles of behavior defining our duties by distinguishing right actions from wrong ones. In contrast, virtue theorists take the central question of ethics as asking, "What kind of person ought we to be?" They see it as their task to identify traits and attitudes reflecting good character and pay careful attention to the role of the affections.

It could be argued that the renewed interest in virtue theory reflects an uneasiness with the sufficiency of moral analysis in which the relevance and contribution of virtue are slighted. The call to virtue, then, may be construed as a summons to displace the focus on conduct in favor of a focus on character. Apparently, this is what G. E. M. Anscombe has urged in her "Modern Moral Philosophy"[6] and Alasdair MacIntyre in his *After Virtue*.[7] Alternatively, the call to virtue may be construed as a plea for balance and comprehensiveness in moral deliberations, the position taken by William Frankena.[8] For my part, I believe that morality cannot be construed within the bounds of principles alone but must also include feelings and attitudes.

Apart from their intrinsic interest, feelings matter also because they often have public or social consequences in action. One consequence of being unforgiving, for instance, is the difficulty of maintaining intimate relationships; another is the fact that the unforgiving person is often vindictive and inclined toward committing acts of revenge.[9] Interestingly enough, John Stuart Mill, an action-theorist, well understood the importance of feelings. He criticized Jeremy Bentham for ignoring character development precisely because he saw that the development of man's affections has consequences for his actions.[10]

What follows from this is that the role of feelings in moral philosophy is philosophically interesting, and to the extent that forgiveness involves feelings, it is interesting as well. It is thus of "very great importance," as Strawson observes, how we analyze "the attitudes and intentions towards us of other human beings, and the great extent to which our personal feelings depend upon, or involve, our beliefs about these attitudes and intentions."[11]

We should then not be surprised that the rebirth of virtue theory has brought in its train an interest in forgiveness, as articles have appeared throughout the journals. Notwithstanding, there is a dearth of literature on the subject generally. While one can only speculate as to why this is so, the most likely explanation is that forgiveness is often thought of as a *Christian* virtue and thus outside the purview of secular philosophers. Ludwig Feuerbach, for instance, argued that forgiveness cannot be accounted for in ordinary moral terms—that it takes us beyond morality and into a religious dimension transcending the ethical.[12] Bishop Joseph Butler, whose writings have a distinctly Christian flavor, is one of the few eminent philosophers to examine forgiveness systematically at all.[13] Even Friedrich Nietzsche, who wrote extensively on resentment (with which forgiveness is connected), argued that Christianity is little more than sublimated *ressentiment*.[14]

Neither did the ancients discuss forgiveness, with the exceptions of Plutarch[15] and Seneca.[16] Nowhere on his intricate list of virtues did Aristotle list the virtue of forgiveness. Forgiveness was given its most prominent expression by Jesus of Nazareth. However, as Hannah Arendt has observed, "The fact that he made this discovery [sic] in a religious context and articulated it in religious language is no reason to take it any less seriously in a strictly secular sense."[17] Aurel Kolnai has taken an even stronger position, arguing that "forgiveness is pre-eminently an ethical subject, and a paper written about it cannot help being a paper in ethics."[18] As I see it, the fact that forgiveness is a religious virtue does not mean that it is necessarily one. The logical separation of morality from religion allows us to examine forgiveness from a moral perspective quite apart from religious dogma.

Having demonstrated the relevance of forgiveness to moral philosophy, my plan for this essay is as follows: In Part I, I will delimit the concept of forgiveness, distinguishing it, in the process, from concepts with which it is related but from which it is logically distinct. I will also propose a model of forgiveness that avoids problems to which others are susceptible. In Part II, I will consider the question of whether and to what extent forgiveness is a virtue. However, before I outline my substantive views, I turn to a consideration of some methodological issues.

William Neblett has argued that "the subject of forgiveness [is] best approached, not with the attempt to define a *concept* (a single *concept* as the meaning of the word), but with the attempt to understand an aspect of our *behavior*, *experience*, of our ongoing moral *practice*."[19] R. J. O'Shaughnessy concurs on this point. As he sees it, "to decide whether any particular case before us can be characterized as a case of forgiveness, we have to pay attention among other things to the way [this] and other expressions are used by the people concerned."[20] What is at issue here is whether an analysis of forgiveness ought to proceed by examining the *meaning* of the term or the *use* of it—the meaning of the *term* or the *speaker's meaning* when he uses the term.

For Neblett and O'Shaughnessy, "forgiveness" cannot be captured in a straitjacket of necessary and sufficient conditions but is best approached by examining features of forgiving behavior, including (but not limited to) speech behavior. The reason for this has not only to do with Neblett's and O'Shaughnessy's linguistic commitments, but also with how nebulous a concept forgiveness is. Joanna North, for instance, has pointed out that, at best, forgiveness is "difficult to define" and, at worst, it is "paradoxical or even impossible" to define.[21] In a similar vein, Uma Narayan has argued that there is not one, but many different concepts of forgiveness.[22]

However, despite the difficulty of defining forgiveness and the methodological counsel of Neblett and O'Shaughnessy, much of the discussion surrounding the subject has presupposed that we *can* define forgiveness and that we can do so by specifying its essential features. Neblett explains, "It is easy to come to this belief particularly if one presumes that saying 'I forgive you' never alone constitutes forgiveness and that therefore there must be features of human behavior, other than speech behavior, that are *essential* to the act of forgiving."[23] But of the models of forgiveness discussed in the literature, none represents a satisfactory analysis. Thus, it may be that, on at least some occasions, "I forgive you" *does* constitute forgiveness. At least, the truth of this claim would go a long way toward explaining why it is that forgiveness is so difficult to define. To quote Neblett:

> *Many philosophers mistakenly assume that the meaning of an expression is always precise and clear in the sense that what the speaker intends when he uses an expression is always precise and clear.* When words are used to describe or to define we know what it means for them to be "precise" and "clear." But when words are used in performatory utterances, the *meanings* of these words are not "precise" and "clear" in this same way, if they can be said to be "precise" and "clear" at all. For the meaning of performatory utterances is linked to the *purpose* for which those utterances are employed, which means that the meaning of performatory utterances is linked to the *intentions* of the speaker-actor who "employs" those utterances.[24]

What follows from this is that it would be a mistake to rule out a priori that "I forgive you" is a performative utterance. With this in mind, I shall argue—against the mainstream of philosophical thought—that saying "I forgive you" can, under appropriate circumstances, perform the verbal magic that Neblett and O'Shaughnessy suggest it can do. At the same time, I shall argue—as they do not—for a paradigm of forgiveness on which its many uses converge and from which they diverge. I believe that, notwithstanding the obscurity of the concept as well as the commitment to meaning as use, we can depict a paradigm of forgiveness that is consonant with our moral attitudes and beliefs. Of course, in depicting this paradigm, I am hardly supposing that the paradigm applies to every case where "I forgive you" is uttered. The notion of a paradigm is consistent with alternative conceptions that manifest a diversity of forms and cover a variety of purposes from context to context. Thus, rather than providing a complete phenomenological account of the complex attitude that constitutes forgiveness, I am offering something more limited in scope. But I do think that "forgiveness" represents a well-entrenched concept, making the task ahead in part the descriptive one of laying it out and bringing it into line with other concepts as well as with experience, linguistic or otherwise.

Finally, it hardly needs saying that, in advancing my thesis, I am not implying that saying "I forgive you" is the *only* way that one can forgive any more than saying "I do" at the altar is the *only* way that one can get married. Just as one can get married (under common law, at least) by living with a person for a number of years, one can forgive by having an attitude of the appropriate kind.

A second methodological issue centers on my distinguishing the nature of forgiveness from the value thereof. Jeffrie Murphy has argued that the question "What is forgiveness?" cannot be distinguished from the question "How is forgiveness a virtue?" As he sees it, the two questions are logically related.[25]

I have two reasons for differing with Murphy. The first concerns the position I take on the question of whether virtue can be displayed in morally bad actions. With the exceptions of Philippa Foot[26] and Peter Geach,[27] no one perceives difficulty in the thought that virtue can be displayed in morally bad actions. George Henrik von Wright, for instance, speaks of the courage of the villain as if this were quite unproblematic.[28] However, although courage is a virtue, it does not follow that it acts as a virtue wherever it is found. Courage does not act as a virtue when the villain turns his courage to evil ends.[29] In saying this, I am not implying that the villain cannot display courage, only that there is nothing praiseworthy in his doing so. So, too, I believe that forgiveness may or may not be praiseworthy, depending on why it is tendered. Thus, to be more precise, it is not as if I think that *virtue* cannot be displayed in morally bad actions; such a claim rings of incoherency. Rather, my claim is that the trait or disposition that is ordinarily a virtue does not count as one when the trait displayed is morally troublesome.

A second reason for differing with Murphy concerns a logical peculiarity of construing forgiveness as a value-laden concept. Murphy defines forgiveness as the overcoming of resentment *on moral grounds*.[30] What follows from this is that one cannot forgive in the absence of a moral reason. But surely we *can* forgive in the absence of a moral reason; we can even forgive for no reason at all.[31] And we can do so without conceptual confusion. To see this, compare "forgiveness" with a clear case of a value-laden term—namely, "murder." I take it we can safely define murder as "the unjustifiable killing of an innocent human being." So defined, it makes no sense to talk of a "justified murder" (as opposed to a justified *killing*); such a phrase is a contradiction in terms. But where a "justified murder" does not make sense, justified forgiveness does. For this reason, it is best to keep the nature and value of forgiveness apart.

Turning, then, to my analysis of forgiveness, what I intend to show is that forgiveness is an attitude that is characteristically expressed in the locution "I forgive you." Assuming, as I do, that an attitude cannot be characterized without referring to the judgments on which it is founded, I shall identify such judgments in an effort to show what it is one does in performing the linguistic act of expressing forgiveness. Thus, I shall argue that, in expressing forgiveness of an agent X for his act A, a speaker S represents as true the following statements:

(1) X did A;
(2) A was wrong;
(3) X was responsible for doing A;
(4) S was personally injured by X's doing A;
(5) S resented being injured by X's doing A; and
(6) S has overcome his resentment for X's doing A, or is at least willing to try to overcome it.

In arguing that the expression of forgiveness is a performative utterance, I oppose the mainstream of philosophers who reject this view. For them, forgiveness is construed, at the very least, as the overcoming of resentment. This implies that, even if one sincerely *says*

"I forgive you," there is no forgiveness until every last ounce of resentment is gone. This is the view taken by Butler, Downie, Murphy, and others. All regard the overcoming of resentment as a necessary, if not sufficient, condition of forgiveness. In my view, while a speaker often implies that resentment has been overcome when he expresses forgiveness, he need not so imply this so long as he implies he is willing to try to overcome it. Furthermore, there is an important difference between what a term implies and what a speaker implies.

Having analyzed forgiveness, my next task will be to examine its nature as a moral response. Working backward from resentment to forgiveness, I will argue that one ought to resent an individual who has done one moral injury—that is, hold the injury against him. Failure to have what Strawson calls the "reactive attitude" of resentment is to convey, emotionally, either that we do not think we have rights or that we do not take our rights seriously.

If, then, there are times when resentment is appropriate, it follows that there are times when it is not and, in spite of an otherwise proclivity to resent, we ought to forgive those who have wronged us. However, it is hardly a virtue to forgive if, in doing so, we deny ourselves our own moral rights. For this reason, I will argue that forgiveness is a virtue, but only if given for a moral reason. Claiming that forgiveness lies within the discretion of the victim, I will argue that it is a virtue when it is permitted by the principles of morality and not ruled out by other considerations. I leave for later an account of what such considerations might be, noting only at this time that a wrongdoer's *repentance* is alone appropriate. Thus, when a speaker S expresses his forgiveness of an agent X for his act A and does so in a way that is a virtue, he represents—in addition to statements (1) through (5)—not (6), but this:

(6*) S has overcome his resentment for X's doing A or is at least willing to try to overcome it, since X has repented his wrongful conduct.

Throughout this essay, I operate on the assumption that we can analyze forgiveness irrespective of its characterization as a religious virtue. There is, to be sure, a great deal of literature (which I largely ignore) that raises interesting questions of theological importance. Anne Minas, for one, has raised the question of whether a divine being can tender forgiveness—that is, whether forgiveness is a response that is even possible for God.[32] As she sees it, a divine being cannot forgive on whatever model of forgiveness is conceptually meaningful.[33] Meirlys Lewis, on the other hand, examines such models and concludes that they do not deny intelligibility to religious discourse at all.[34]

For John Gingell, "the only tenable position for the theist who wishes to claim the possibility of [divine] forgiveness is an acceptance of the first horn of the *Euthyphro* dilemma," which to him is unacceptable.[35] In arguing against the possibility of divine forgiveness, Gingell examines the logic of the verb "to forgive" and concludes that it, like the verb "to promise," can only meaningfully be uttered on behalf of oneself and not on behalf of someone else.[36] Fyodor Dostoyevsky makes a similar point in *The Brothers Karamazov* when he has Ivan Karamazov argue that God lacks "standing" to forgive another's misconduct. As he sees it, only the injured party is in a position to forgive.[37] Both, however, tacitly deny that an injury to man is not also an injury to God—a position I do not share.

Herbert Morris, while not defending per se a theological conception, ascribes to forgiveness a religious dimension.[38] He sees forgiveness as a process, akin to growing flowers, in which there are acts we can take to "till the soil and sow the seed . . . so that forgiveness may more probably burst into bloom"[39] but which does not come about by human agency alone. Thus, not unlike flowers, which require other causes to "burst into bloom" ("the sun and the rain if you will"),[40] forgiveness requires "grace" and "mystery" for it to come about. It is, then, on Morris's conception, "independent of our will, even though . . . 'an intimation of agency' is present."[41]

For my part, I see no problem extending what I have to say about forgiveness to theological discussions of the subject. Assuming, as I do, the truth of Aquinas's "doctrine of analogy" (according to which the terms we employ apply to God *in some sense* at least),[42] I see no problem in God forgiving man in situations analogous to man's forgiving man. Furthermore, in assuming this doctrine, I see the justification of divine forgiveness as analogous to the justification of human forgiveness.

In conclusion, what I hope to achieve in examining forgiveness is a philosophical exploration of its nature and value. It hardly needs saying that I wish to avoid sermonizing. I make this explicit only because forgiveness is a subject tending to elicit respectful piety rather than serious philosophical thought. In spite of the Christian tinge of the subject, I am convinced that forgiveness is worthy of engaging the attention of moral philosophers, Christian and non-Christian. To that end, what follows is an investigation of the subject in what is best characterized as an essay in moral philosophy.

Part I

What Forgiveness Is and Is Not

1

What Forgiveness Is Not

The question "What is forgiveness?" has largely been ignored by moral philosophers working outside the confines of a religious context. Where it has been discussed, forgiveness has been thought particularly difficult to define. I shall discuss some of these difficulties and propose a conception that, while surprising, does justice to the concept in a way that competing conceptions do not.

Before I begin, it will be helpful to bear in mind first that when an agent forgives, he forgives a wrongdoer *for* an injury received.[1] To paraphrase Antony Flew's remark about punishment, forgiveness is *of* an offender *for* an offense against the forgiver.[2] Thus, though we will have occasion to speak of one person forgiving another, we should understand that the one person forgives the other for the wrongful act that caused the injury. I make this explicit because Jesus, for one, sometimes speaks of forgiving not only people but also their actions, where the latter is specifically compared to the absolving of a debt. In this sense, forgiving an action is preparatory to forgiving an agent. When the victim "sends away" the wrongful act in the way that a creditor absolves a debt, he no longer holds the wrongful act against the wrongdoer, in the way that a creditor no longer holds the debt against the debtor.[3] Strictly speaking, it is the agent, not the action, that is the object of forgiveness.[4]

The second point to bear in mind is that forgiveness is *unilateral*. The wrongdoer need not be involved in any way for forgiveness to occur. Again, I make this explicit because P. F. Strawson, for one, maintains that to ask for forgiveness is "partly to acknowledge that the attitude displayed in our action was such as might properly be resented; partly to repudiate that attitude. To forgive is to accept the repudiation, to forswear the resentment."[5] And while we should not take Strawson as offering a comprehensive analysis of the concept, it is, as given, open to the objection that forgiveness is bilateral in the sense specified. It is possible, for instance, to forgive a person where that person has not repudiated his attitude—where, for example, that person has died.[6]

With this in mind, my discussion of forgiveness begins by considering what it is that forgiveness is not. Of course, there are countless things forgiveness is not; my concern is with models of forgiveness that, for one reason or another, do not stand up to analysis.

Forgiveness as the Reversal of Moral Judgment

It may be thought that forgiveness is the retraction or modification of a previous moral judgment made of a wrongful act that one has committed. Anne Minas gives us an example:

> The eloping couple might be forgiven in this way by their parents. The parents, in their shock and dismay when first hearing the news, censure the action harshly. Later, however, they realize that their judgment about the elopement was too severe and so they modify or abandon it, and so forgive the couple.[7]

Now, it is easy to see why forgiveness cannot be construed along these lines once we realize that elopement is not wrong (or not *very* wrong). Since, as I shall argue in Chapter 2, in forgiving a person we represent that what the person did *was* wrong, the expression of forgiveness by the parents of this couple is incoherent. Thus, although we sometimes express forgiveness because new facts that affect our assessment of the situation have come to light, the expression of forgiveness in the absence of real wrongdoing cannot be countenanced as forgiveness at all.

The situation is appreciably changed, however, if a son, for example, asks his parents to reverse their censure of his having murdered his sister. Here, the act in question *is* wrong. Now if, in expressing their forgiveness, the parents represent that their previous adverse moral judgment about the act in question is retracted, then—if what they mean by this is that the act was not really wrong—their expression of forgiveness is once again incoherent. The parents may *believe* that what their son did was not really wrong if they somehow manage to believe this is true, but the falsity of this belief would not be in question. Thus, while one can, in expressing forgiveness, represent the belief that the act is not wrong,[8] it is true belief that is presupposed by forgiveness.

A rather different version of this model is the one employed by Jean Hampton, who argues that forgiveness is not the modification of a previous adverse moral judgment about the *act* that was committed, but about the *agent* who committed the act.

> Forgiveness is . . . the decision to see a wrongdoer in a new, more favorable light. Nor is this decision in any way a condonation of wrong. The forgiver never gives up her opposition to the wrongdoer's action, nor does she even give up her opposition to the wrongdoer's bad character traits. Instead, she revises her judgment of the person himself—where the person is understood to be something other than or more than the character traits of which she does not approve.[9]

Ostensibly, Hampton is assuming an ethics of "being" according to which a person's moral worth is determined by something more than the sum total of what he does, which position is attributable to an ethics of "doing."[10] In the former view, the moral worth of a person is determined by appealing to his characteristic pattern of action. Thus, if a person is judged good, then isolated episodes of immoral conduct are downplayed so long as there is evidence that the person in question is otherwise moral. So, too, if a person is judged evil, then isolated episodes of moral conduct are downplayed so long as there is evidence that the person in question is otherwise immoral.

It is beyond the scope of this discussion to assess the relative merits of an ethics of being as opposed to an ethics of doing. What is within its scope is a particular objection that is sometimes leveled against proponents of virtue theory, and that I find is valid against them. This objection is the epistemological one that we cannot know, with any degree of certainty, who really is virtuous and who is not other than by appealing to a person's behavior. However, this is precisely what the virtue theorist wants to deny in focusing, as he does, on paradigmatic individuals—which is his starting point for developing a moral theory.

The standard strategy for meeting this objection is to maintain that we can infer a person's character by observing his conduct. However, this will not do, if only because virtue theorists are committed to the view that the relationship between who a person is and what a person does is a contingent rather than necessary one. However, if this is so—that is, if a person's moral worth is not wholly derivable from the actions to which it gives rise—then a person's character is something "spiritual." But if a person's character is something spiritual, it follows that it cannot be observed, which brings us back to the question of how it is that we can recognize a virtuous person other than by what he does.[11]

Applying this objection to Hampton's model, the question we must ask is this: In precisely what sense can a wrongdoer be understood to be something more than the actions or character traits of which we disapprove without committing ourselves to a dubious ontology? Hampton says, "To forgive someone for an action or trait is a way of removing it as evidence of the state of his soul."[12] Taken literally, this model invites epistemological problems that are more troublesome than the problems her model is designed to avoid. Taken metaphorically, this model reduces itself to the claim that a person's character is wholly derivable from the actions he performs—thus undermining its very foundation. For these reasons, it will simply not do to argue that forgiveness is the modification of a judgment about a person's character rather than about the acts to which it allegedly gives rise.

There are, to be sure, other problems with Hampton's position, not the least of which is her contention that forgiveness involves a "decision to see a wrongdoer in a new, more favorable light."[13] It is quite reasonable to ask how it is that one can *decide* to see a person other than what he is without engaging in self-deception. If Jones resents Smith, Jones will naturally see Smith as vicious. However, as Hampton would have it, Jones can *decide* to see Smith as virtuous. Notwithstanding the epistemological problems associated with "willing to believe" what one does not,[14] it is not at all clear how we can avoid the moral problems associated with believing what one does not. Thus, Hampton's model fares little better than the one that construes forgiveness to be the modification of an adverse moral judgment about the act the wrongdoer has committed.

Forgiveness as the Remission of Punishment

Rather than consisting of the reversal of moral judgment, it may be thought that forgiveness consists of the remission of punishment where "punishment" is used primarily, though not exclusively, in the legal sense of the term. The Oxford English Dictionary, for one, encourages this view. One definition the OED gives is "to remit, to let off, to pardon." In this connection, it mentions Hobbes's "An Authority to

Forgive or Retain Sins," which does seem to equate forgiveness with punishment-remission.[15]

Now, as Anne Minas observes, sometimes punishment is remitted because of a new, more favorable judgment about the moral aspects of the case at hand. These include cases where special circumstances merit a special kind of judgment about the action, to the effect that what was done was not really wrong.[16] But these are simply cases of forming judgments where all relevant circumstances are considered, and are thus inapplicable to the forgiveness situation.[17] However, there are also cases where punishment is remitted without reversing or modifying a moral judgment about the wrongdoing the punishment was supposed to be punishment for. Does the remission of punishment in these types of cases amount to forgiveness? There are several reasons to think not. Some of these reasons are taken up by R. J. O'Shaughnessy's "Forgiveness," where he is concerned with refuting what he dubs the "RP thesis"—that is, the view that equates forgiveness with the remission of punishment.[18]

According to O'Shaughnessy, there are three versions of the RP thesis. In its strong form, it asserts a straightforward identity between forgiveness and punishment-remission. In the first of its weak forms, it asserts that punishment-remission is a necessary condition of forgiveness; and in the second of its weak forms, it asserts that punishment-remission is a sufficient condition of forgiveness. The difference is that the first of the weak forms precludes statements like "I'll not punish you although I can't forgive you," while the second precludes statements like "I'll forgive you, but just the same I'll have to punish you." The difference between these and the strong form is that the weaker forms explain the *definiendum* in terms of the *definiens* plus something else. One position invites us to understand forgiveness as the remission of punishment with something added; the other invites us to understand the remission of punishment as forgiveness with something added.[19]

As O'Shaughnessy sees it, "the most obvious objection to all these positions is that, since they entail the impossibility of statements which are frequently made, and which are perfectly intelligible, they must be false by reduction."[20] We speak, for instance, about letting people off while at the same time being unable to forgive them. So, too, punishments are sometimes imposed, because the law prescribes them, when in fact it makes sense to say that the victim has forgiven the wrongdoer.

Another objection O'Shaughnessy raises is that there are certain instances of forgiving behavior where the question of punishment just does not arise. He mentions forgiving an old friend for a piece of thoughtless behavior. Here, it would be odd to insist that, in so doing, we are remitting him a punishment; we may never have intended to punish him at all.[21]

Still another objection to the RP thesis is that forgiveness essentially involves two conditions that do not necessarily apply to cases of punishment-remission. First, according to O'Shaughnessy, there must be some kind of personal relationship between forgiver and wrongdoer. Second, part of what is meant by saying someone has forgiven somebody is that the forgiver has undergone a certain change of attitude. The absence of the first condition accounts for our belief that it is inappropriate to characterize as forgiveness the pardoning of an offender by an official.[22] The mere satisfaction of the second condition shows that forgiveness can take place independently of punishment-remission. We could then say (according to O'Shaughnessy) that, although in certain kinds of cases the attitude of forgiveness is expressed by the remission of punishment, this is a contingent matter—which establishes the logical independence of the concepts in question.[23]

Forgiveness as the Overcoming of Resentment

Another—and more formidable—model of forgiveness is as the overcoming of resentment. This is the model to which Bishop Joseph Butler subscribed.[24] Butler was concerned with the question of how a loving God could implant in us so unloving a passion as resentment. Prima facie, at least, resentment appears to be a passion that is unambiguously evil. However, as Butler saw it, the reason why resentment arouses suspicion is that it is often directed at trivial affronts (as opposed to real moral injury) and sometimes provokes untoward behavior (such as vigilantism). Nietzsche, for one, called attention to the fact that the retributive urge rests on resentment.[25] But to Butler, what is not consistent with a gospel of love is to be dominated by resentment and act unjustly on it. The passion itself is not condemnable. Thus, Butler saw forgiveness (the overcoming of resentment) as a virtue that serves to check resentment and keep it within its proper bounds.[26]

Other more contemporary philosophers have followed Butler in construing forgiveness as the overcoming of resentment. Kathleen Dean Moore, for instance, says that "the attitude of forgiveness is characterized by the presence of good will or by the lack of personal resentment for the injury."[27] A. C. Ewing said that forgiveness is the "right state of feeling and a right mental disposition towards the man who has wronged you, especially in the laying aside of personal resentment."[28] Martin Hughes defined forgiveness as "the cancellation of deserved hostilities and the substitution of friendlier attitudes."[29] R. S. Downie, whose essay "Forgiveness" served as the focal point of a discussion of the subject in the 1960s, maintained that forgiveness is characterized by the absence of resentment and the presence of *agape*.[30]

Recently, Jeffrie Murphy expanded this conception by arguing that forgiveness is not merely the overcoming of resentment, but the overcoming of resentment *on moral grounds*.[31] Murphy's problem is this: If forgiveness is the overcoming of resentment *simpliciter*, then—by implication—any time resentment is overcome, forgiveness may be said to have taken place. However, as Murphy sees it, there are cases where one has overcome resentment but we would hesitate to say that one has forgiven. We can, argues Murphy, simply forget the fact that an injury has occurred.[32] In this sense, "forgive and forget" is not redundant. We can also take measures to remove resentment, should such resentment poison our lives. We can, for instance, enlist psychiatric help in an effort to gain peace of mind. But—Murphy says—such cases of natural and therapeutic forgetting could not possibly count as cases of forgiveness, if only because forgiveness is a virtue and there is nothing virtuous about these cases.[33] Because of this, Murphy construes forgiveness to be the overcoming of resentment, but only if tendered on moral grounds.

In the Introduction, I have mentioned my reasons for thinking Murphy to be wrong in his conception of forgiveness. What is important here is the way in which Murphy's account differs from those discussed above. While it is not entirely clear, it appears that, in one view (the one attributed to Butler, Moore, Ewing, and Hughes), the overcoming of resentment is a necessary and sufficient condition of forgiveness. In another (Murphy's), the overcoming of resentment is a necessary but not sufficient condition of forgiveness. I shall later explore some difficulties with both of these conditional aspects; but before I do that, it will help to examine still other views that differ in important respects.

H. J. N. Horsbrugh, while essentially agreeing that forgiveness is the overcoming of resentment, suggests a refinement based on his belief that forgiveness is a *process*.[34]

> The main difference between the view that I have been putting forward and that advanced by Downie [and Butler, Moore, Ewing, Hughes, and Murphy] lies in my insistence that forgiveness is normally a process of some duration, and that, even when the forgiving party's actions are uniformly benevolent, he or she cannot be said to have carried this process to completion until the negative feelings engendered by the injury have been eliminated.[35]

It is instructive to pay attention to Horsbrugh's reasons for thinking that forgiveness is a process. As mentioned, Horsbrugh does believe that the overcoming of resentment is a necessary and sufficient condition of forgiveness. However, defining forgiveness in this manner leaves open the question of whether the overcoming of resentment is a process or an event brought about by some inner act of will. Forgiveness as an event is the view attributed to Downie, and may arguably be implied by others as well.

According to Horsbrugh, however, there are good reasons for thinking that forgiveness is not an event that can be carried to fruition immediately, through an act of will. While it is theoretically possible to forgive a person through an act of will, the overcoming of resentment normally takes place over some length of time. In the view he rejects, we forgive another when we will away our resentment; but in reality—more often than not—our resentment persists long after the decision is made not to harbor it. It is not uncommon to brood over an injury long after we have willed it away. The wife, for instance, who has forgiven her husband for keeping a mistress, may will away her resentment only to have it resurface on seeing "the other woman" several years later.

Now what are we to make of such common occurrences? One solution is to say that we have not forgiven, though we thought that we did. Forgiveness takes place only when one has *entirely* purged oneself of the sense of injury, and this takes place over a certain length of time. For this reason, Horsbrugh distinguishes between acting in ways that express good-will, which he sees as the beginning of forgiveness, and overcoming our resentment—that is, forgiveness proper. Thus, Horsbrugh writes,

> the decision to forgive is normally only the beginning of a process of forgiveness that may take a considerable time to complete. Indeed, there are cases in which it is never completed, even though one is committed to completing it once the decision to forgive has been made. For this reason, forgiveness may be said normally to have two aspects: (i) A

> volitional aspect—that which is involved in the decision to forgive, a decision which can usually be partially implemented at once by acting with good-will towards one's injurer; and (ii) an emotional aspect—that which has to do with the extirpation of such negative feelings as those of anger, resentment, and hostility. In the view that I am taking the process of forgiveness is not completed until one has entirely rid oneself of the sense of injury.[36]

The main reason Horsbrugh distinguishes between what he calls the "volitional aspect of forgiveness" and the "emotional aspect" is the point we express in the colloquial phrase "trying to forgive." "It would be inappropriate," he maintains, "to speak of 'trying to forgive' if forgiveness were simply a matter of acting in ways that express good-will towards one's injurer for that is always in the immediate power of the moral agent."[37] In this respect, he agrees with Murphy that forgiveness is "primarily concerned with how one feels instead of how one acts."[38]

Apparently, the main difference between Horsbrugh and the position he is arguing against is not so much what forgiveness is, but rather when it is that forgiveness occurs. In the one view, forgiveness occurs when the forgiver decides that he will no longer harbor resentment—that is, when the decision is made not to resent. In the other view, since it sometimes happens that resentment appears after the decision has been made to drive it out by an act of will, forgiveness is seen as a process that is completed when negative feelings no longer persist.

At this point, we should pause to consider the merits of both Horsbrugh's position and the one he opposes. It is true, as Horsbrugh observes, that resentment sometimes appears long after the decision to forgive has been made, and for this reason cannot be construed as an act of will alone. Of course, much depends on the relationship of the parties (e.g., whether it is intimate and continuous or distant and temporary); on the culpability of the wrongdoer (e.g., whether the injury was deliberate or negligent); and on the magnitude of the injury.[39] The same resentment that is spontaneously reversed between friends may linger or disappear and resurface between colleagues. To the extent that Butler, Ewing, Hughes, and others subscribe to a conception of forgiveness as a moment of will, then, Horsbrugh's criticism is valid.

But does Horsbrugh's conception fare any better? As I see it, we can decide to forgive, act benevolently toward our injurer, and yet be mistaken in believing we have overcome our resentment. It is a psychological truism that certain feelings—particularly negative ones such as resentment—tend to be suppressed only to resurface later. Thus, rather than correcting for the objections he has raised against construing forgiveness as the overcoming of resentment spontaneously at will, Horsbrugh merely *delays* them. Furthermore, it is also a psychological truism that feelings resurface in unusual guises. Psychologists often speak of the phenomenon of "reaction formation," which is what happens when an angry or resentful person suppresses his anger and then acts in exceedingly kind ways. It is precisely this phenomenon that sometimes makes us wary of people who are "too nice." Then, too, there is the phenomenon of "projection": attributing to another person an emotion that one has oneself. Thus, "he is angry," sometimes means "I am angry." And all of this notwithstanding the fact that we are often unaware of the feelings we harbor. The point is that, in all of these cases, resentment *is* present, and so it will not do simply to say that forgiveness is a process rather than an act of will. In either view, resentment that manifests following what was believed to be forgiveness undermines the claim that forgiveness has occurred.

The main motivation behind Horsbrugh's thesis is his insistence that forgiveness cannot be impermanent. As Horsbrugh puts it,

> complete forgiveness is always taken to be permanent and . . . any appearances to the contrary are attributed to the infliction of a second injury or to the discovery that the first was much more reprehensible than the injured party has hitherto supposed. It is part of the logic of the term "forgiveness," then, that to forgive is to forgive permanently.[40]

Thus, suppose that Jack commits an act of violence against Jill for which Jill forgives him, and that at some later date he does it again, resulting in a second injury. Suppose further that in the ensuing quarrel Jill brings up the earlier incident. Does this mean that Jill's forgiveness was impermanent? As Horsbrugh sees it, either Jill had not really forgiven Jack for the earlier injury (so that a further injury would be expected to arouse her latent resentment), or she is responding to a different and more serious injury—such as Jack's attacking her again after having promised never to do so.[41] In either case, Horsbrugh's "complete forgiveness" is the starting point of analysis.

There are two objections to this analysis, however. If, by definition, forgiveness is permanent, then Jill's current resentment must indeed mean that either she did not forgive Jack for the first attack or she is responding to the second attack and not the first. This would be an analytic truth. But why insist that forgiveness is permanent by definition? Certainly, we cannot parse psychological states in the rather facile manner to which Horsbrugh refers. Feelings do not come so neatly assembled, which makes Horsbrugh's analysis rather ad hoc. Furthermore, Horsbrugh's appeal to "complete" forgiveness invites us to believe that a person can be forgiven "incompletely." Now, if such "incomplete forgiveness" means that the process of forgiveness has not been carried to fruition, then we can raise no objection to Horsbrugh's inverse "complete forgiveness." Certainly, we do sometimes say that we have not completely forgiven one who has injured us, but we could also say, with a slight ellipsis, that we have not "really" or "truly" forgiven. Thus we are inexorably led to distinguish between forgiveness on the one hand and *true* forgiveness on the other—a distinction that is hardly illuminating.[42]

To see this more clearly, consider that according to Horsbrugh's analysis the statement "Jones forgives Smith" is true if and only if Jones harbors no ill-will at all toward Smith. It follows that, should Jones harbor even the slightest amount of resentment toward Smith, such resentment will falsify the claim that Jones has in fact forgiven Smith. But surely, the condition of having overcome *all* resentment is too strong a condition to impose on forgiveness. We quite naturally count as instances of forgiveness certain behaviors that accommodate *some* resentment. We may say, for instance, that Jones has forgiven Smith, when really we know that Jones bears some ill-will toward Smith. Since this is so, then forgiveness cannot *mean*—cannot be equated with—the overcoming of resentment.

Thus, something has surely gone amiss if, in explicating forgiveness, we are forced to distinguish what it is from what it *really* is. Certainly, the standard we usually employ for the application of a term is the average of the kind. We call a man tall, for instance, if he is above the average human height. We do not say that Jones is short (or not *really* tall) because he is shorter than a tree, or that someone is a bad student because his answer to a question on his exam is worse than that given by the very best student.[43] Why, then, should we insist they fail to forgive their wrongdoers until such time as all their resentment is permanently eliminated? We cannot, as I have argued, even be sure of this as an accomplished fact. The real problem, or so I shall argue, is the insistence in the first place that the overcoming of resentment is a necessary condition of forgiveness at all.[44]

This latter criticism is not directed exclusively at Horsbrugh. It is applicable to any construction of forgiveness that takes the overcoming of resentment to be a necessary condition of the forgiving response. There are, however, other problems that *are* unique to Horsbrugh. Given his thesis that forgiveness is a process of some unknown duration, it then becomes impossible to distinguish the process of forgiving from cases of forgetting.[45] We have already seen that forgiving and forgetting are logically distinct. Furthermore—and again this is true not only for Horsbrugh—defining forgiveness as the overcoming of resentment results in an asymmetry between forgiving and *being forgiven*. If, for instance, a person represents that he has forgiven his wrongdoer (either by willing away his resentment or by completing a process), we would naturally say that the wrongdoer is forgiven. But suppose the resentment surfaces again at some later date, or never quite vanishes but assumes a different form. It would follow that the wrongdoer is not forgiven, however reasonably the wrongdoer may think otherwise. There is something disconcerting in even acknowledging that one may believe oneself to have been forgiven when in fact one has not been.[46] We want, I believe, a conception of forgiveness such that a wrongdoer is forgiven when his victim forgives him, without all the complications that attach to the positions we are now considering.

Perhaps the main reason for this asymmetry is that, as Jean Hampton puts it, "we typically think of forgiveness as an act that is 'directed' at the wrongdoer, and not merely some kind of internal emotional change inside the victim."[47] Hampton also remarks, "One who is supposed to have experienced a 'change of heart' towards a wrongdoer but still finds the prospect of associating with the wrongdoer disturbing has probably not succeeded in forgiving the wrongdoer."[48] What the asymmetry suggests is that the overcoming of resentment is not quite enough to fix the definition of forgiveness at all.

In summary, we have seen that, in most acccounts of forgiveness, the overcoming of resentment is thought to be a necessary condition, while some see it as a sufficient one as well. In one view, the overcoming of resentment is apparently a matter of willing it away; while in another, it is a process that takes place over an unspecified period of time. We have taken note of the various problems that arise if forgiveness is construed according to either of these models. Both views lead us to distinguish between forgiveness and *true* forgiveness—a consequence, I have urged, that is far from satisfactory. They also lead to an asymmetry between forgiving and being forgiven. (We might say, to paraphrase Solon, that the motto of both views' proponents is this: "Call no man forgiven until the forgiver is dead.") We have seen that, in at least Horsbrugh's account, we are hard pressed to distinguish cases of forgiving from cases of forgetting (natural or therapeutic). We can add to this the fact that hardly any of our theorists has been concerned with the *behavior* the forgiver might be expected to exhibit, having forgiven his wrongdoer. Horsbrugh does pay homage to the benevolent actions that a wrongdoer is entitled to receive once the decision has been made to forgive him; but like the others, Horsbrugh essentially ignores this aspect of forgiveness as it pertains to the forgiver. Horsbrugh's analysis is rather like Murphy's, who maintains that forgiveness is primarily about how one feels, and like Kathleen Dean Moore's, who admits that when a wrongdoer has been forgiven he "expects certain characteristic ways of acting . . . but unless a change of attitude follows or accompanies the words 'I forgive you,' no forgiving can be said to have taken place."[49]

Finally, I would be remiss if I did not make mention of Norvin Richards's conception of forgiveness, according to which forgiveness consists not in the overcoming of resentment alone, but in the overcoming of every negative feeling (contempt, sadness, disappointment, etc.) that a victim might feel on having been injured.[50] While I shall later expound on Richards's position, suffice it to say here that, even if we widen the scope of feelings an individual must overcome in order to forgive, the same objections applicable to forgiveness as the overcoming of resentment apply, pari passu, to forgiveness construed as the overcoming of all negative feelings.[51]

Forgiveness as No Thing

While models of forgiveness that take the overcoming of resentment to constitute its essence (in one form or another) are the most renowned and the most worthy of respect, there are, as we have seen, other models deserving of attention. One we have not yet discussed is advanced by Joseph Beatty, who employs as *paradeigma* Jean-Paul Sartre's analysis of "Concrete Relations of Others" in the latter's *Being and Nothingness*.[52]

According to Beatty, the main problem with most accounts of forgiveness is in seeing it as some kind of *thing* that gets transmitted from the forgiver to the wrongdoer. "When we speak of 'asking for forgiveness' and 'granting forgiveness,' it is easy enough to slip into the error of believing that forgiveness, because it is often expressed verbally or by means of a visible token of some kind, is something transmitted from one person to another."[53] However, as Beatty views it, forgiveness is not a *thing* that is given over as if it were a commodity. And while we do sometimes speak as though a person lacked forgiveness at one moment but was given it at another, such language is conceptually confused. When one asks to be forgiven and another does forgive, there is no forgiveness that has been given any more than, as Augustine observed, a lover gives his love to his beloved. Love is not a thing that is given in the same sense that one gives a gift.

But if forgiveness is not a thing for Beatty, what is it? What does one want when asking for forgiveness, and what does one give when giving forgiveness? Drawing on Sartre, Beatty answers to this effect: When asking for forgiveness, what we want, essentially, is that the injured party not see us in the way we are presently seen—as morally responsible agents who are blameworthy. The project of asking for forgiveness is designed to get the injured party to see the wrongdoer in the way that the wrongdoer sees himself—as an agent who is not to be identified solely with the accusing image the injured party has of him. In "giving" forgiveness, the injured party represents to his wrongdoer his *own* fault in seeing the agent as identical with the wrong committed, and his own wish to be forgiven for his blindness.[54] Beatty puts it this way:

> In attempting to make the other [the injured party] see him as forgiveable, and thereby give her his forgiveness of himself, he actually succeeds in transmitting to her a recognition of her own fault in accusing and rejecting him. What he gives her, therefore, is not his forgiveness but his asking for forgiveness. He cannot give her *her forgiveness*, though that is what he is after. Nor can he give her, in the final analysis, his forgiveness of himself. He can only give her his seeking for forgiveness, and she can only give it back to him.[55]

I have little to say about Beatty's analysis except that it works—if it works—only with the Sartrian model on which it is dependent. Whether that model succeeds or fails is well beyond the scope of this discussion. In any event, we do not *need* a Sartrian model to make sense of forgiveness.

Forgiveness as Many Things

At the opposite extreme from forgiveness as no thing—the position put forth by Beatty—there is a more formidable school of thought that sees forgiveness as many things. Represented here are William Neblett[56] and R. J. O'Shaughnessy.[57] In this view, forgiveness can be construed as the overcoming of resentment, but this is only one *kind* of forgiveness. The other kinds of things forgiveness can be are precisely those things specified in dictionaries. Sometimes when one forgives, one is reversing a moral judgment. Other times, one is remitting a punishment. What forgiveness is at any one time depends, then, on what one means when granting it.

Rather than inquiring into the *absolute* meaning of forgiveness in the sense of looking for its necessary and sufficient conditions, this view focuses on what people mean when they *use* the term. This approach, associated with Ludwig Wittgenstein, sees the meaning of a word in terms of its use in language. One does not give an adequate explanation of the meaning of a word simply by describing *how* it is used in language, however; one must still explain what the term is used *for*.[58] And according to both Neblett and O'Shaughnessy, we put the term "forgiveness" to a variety of uses and know what these uses designate by paying attention to how people act, their tone of voice, and the other things they say at the time and subsequently.[59]

To illustrate, O'Shaughnessy cites Shakespeare's *The Tempest*, in which Shakespeare has Prospero tell Sebastian,

> For you, most wicked sir, whom to call brother would even infect my mouth, I do forgive Thy rankest faults.[60]

From the context of the play, O'Shaughnessy is convinced that Prospero's intention in expressing his forgiveness is to call off the demons whom he has caused to torment the usurper of his dukedom. This being so, he is using the term "forgiveness" to mean the forgoing of retaliation.[61] But, as O'Shaughnessy sees it, one need not put the term to this use alone. One can even, for instance, use "forgiveness" as a *means* of retaliation. One sees this, for example, when Dorothea in George Eliot's *Middlemarch* realizes that she has offended her husband, Casaubon, and asks to be forgiven.

> "I am glad that you feel that, my dear," Casaubon replied, but there was still an uneasy feeling in his eyes as he looked at her.
>
> "But do you forgive me?" said Dorothea, with a quick sob. "Would not love see returning penitence afar off, and fall on its neck and kiss it?"
>
> "My dear Dorothea—'Who with repentance is not satisfied, is not of heaven and earth':—do you not think me worthy to be banished by that

> severe sentence," said Mr. Casaubon, exerting himself to make a strong statement, and also to smile faintly.
>
> Dorothea was silent, but a tear which had come up with the sob would insist on falling.
>
> "You are excited, my dear. And I also am feeling some unpleasant consequences of too much mental disturbance," said Mr. Casaubon.

And later:

> "I think it is time for us to dress," he added, looking at his watch. They both rose, and there was never any further allusion between them to what had passed on this day.
>
> But Dorothea remembered it to the last with the vividness with which we all remember epochs in our experience when some dear expectation dies, or some new motive is born. Today she had begun to see that she had been under a wild illusion in expecting a response to her feeling from Mr. Casaubon.[62]

According to O'Shaughnessy, it is clear from this extract that Mr. Casaubon is neither willing away his resentment nor forgoing retaliation. In quite a deliberate way, what he is doing *is* retaliating: hurting Dorothea back for the injury she inflicted on him.[63] What follows from this and other examples is that, in the eyes of O'Shaughnessy, the meaning of forgiveness cannot be captured in a straitjacket of necessary and sufficient conditions—a method implied by Butler, Murphy, Downie, and others. What forgiveness means can be determined only by focusing on what people mean when they use the term. Neblett laments at the end of his article, "It is a curious point that some of the genuine insights of Wittgenstein have not been more clearly understood and more sympathetically applied by contemporary moral philosophers."[64]

O'Shaughnessy does not, in fact, demonstrate that forgiveness means many things depending on what people mean when they put the term to use. To say that Prospero uses "forgiveness" to mean that he will forgo retaliation, or that Casaubon uses the term to enable him to retaliate, may only prove that neither Prospero nor Casaubon is using the term correctly, or that, even if they are using the term correctly, they are using it idiosyncratically. Furthermore, if they are using the term idiosyncratically, this implies that their uses have features in common with nonidiosyncratic uses—which is another way of saying that their uses leave room for the convergence on, and divergence from, a paradigm. As Michael Dummet has observed in commenting on Wittgenstein's approach to meaning, Wittgenstein is not saying that an adequate explanation of the meaning of a word is given simply by describing its usage—that is, simply by stating the circumstances in which we make use of the term and those in which we do not. We must still explain the *point* of using the term—that is, explain what it is used *for*. And if we fail to perceive this aspect, we do not understand the point of Wittgenstein's doctrine.[65] Thus, even if O'Shaughnessy's examples succeed in describing ways in which we make use of the term "forgiveness," further analysis is nonetheless required.

To be sure, there are in the literature still other models of what forgiveness is. Aurel Kolnai, for one, sometimes equates forgiving with "re-accepting."[66] However, forgiveness cannot be equated with reacceptance if only because some wrongdoers were not accepted to begin with; that is, there is no relationship to reestablish. It should, then, be clear by now that all of these models are deficient in one way or another. Our own model must therefore respond to these deficiencies: We need a model that avoids the problems others present, and yet satisfies our intuitions about what forgiveness is.

2

What Forgiveness Is

It is easy to believe, as previously demonstrated, that the meaning of forgiveness can be captured in its necessary and sufficient conditions if one simply presumes that saying "I forgive you" never alone constitutes forgiveness. However, it should be clear by now that down this path lies frustration. The elusiveness of the concept can scarcely escape our attention once we give it prolonged scrutiny. Thus, rather than inquiring into the meaning of forgiveness, I propose to examine what it is one does when one performs the linguistic act of expressing forgiveness. John L. Austin's doctrine of performative utterances is unusually helpful for the task at hand.[1]

The locution "I forgive you" belongs to the class of what Austin called "behabitives."[2] "Behabitives," he says in *How to Do Things with Words*, "include the notion of reaction to other people's behavior and fortunes and of attitudes and expressions of attitudes to someone else's past conduct or imminent conduct."[3] For examples of attitudinal expressions that are behabitives, Austin mentions "don't mind," "applaud," "commend," and "approve," among others.[4]

Austin had special misgivings about behabitives; they are, as he puts it, "troublesome because they seem too miscellaneous altogether."[5] However, his comments do not point us in the most helpful (i.e., unequivocal) direction toward understanding them. Austin uses two ideas in order to explicate the concept: on the one hand, that of "adopting" or "taking up" an attitude; and, on the other hand, that of "expressing" or "exhibiting" an attitude.[6] Now the first idea is not very helpful. The taking up or adopting of an attitude does not seem to be a performative at all, having no essential reference to language. However, the second idea—that of expressing or exhibiting a state of mind—seems promising.[7]

Using this approach, we must ask whether there is in fact a locution that includes the term "forgiveness," in the uttering of which the speaker is expressing a state of mind. The answer is that there is such a locution: "I forgive you." It seems natural to assert that in saying "I forgive you," I am expressing ——— toward you for this action, where the blank would be filled in by a word or phrase referring to my state of mind. This, then, is the essential way in which the locution is used. The speaker's primary intention in forgiving someone for an action by using the first-person form of speech is typically to show that he regards the object of the forgiveness in a certain light or has certain feelings about him, rather than to deliver a more impersonal verdict.[8]

Austin admits that "there are obvious connections with both stating or describing what our feelings are, and expressing in the sense of venting our feelings, though behabitives are distinct from both of these."[9] Consider, for instance, the locution "I love you." Construed one way, this sentence is a *report* of how the speaker feels; but construed another way, this sentence *expresses* the feeling the speaker has at the time. This should come as no surprise, since we know that what a speaker means in utilizing an expression is tied up with the situation he is in, his purpose in speaking, who the listener is, and so forth. Furthermore, the sentence "I love you" need not be uttered to express the speaker's feelings. It can be used to manipulate behavior, as well. The point is that, just as "I love you" *can* express a feeling rather than report it, so, too, can "I forgive you" do the same. Similar results obtain when we consider the angry schoolmaster (to use Gilbert Ryle's example) who vents his anger by shouting at the small boy who has just made an arithmetical mistake, "Seven times seven equals forty-nine!"

Let us, then, consider an example that might prove instructive. Consider the following sequence of events in the lives of two friends, John and Mary. At some point in the past, John offended Mary, and afterward, Mary said to John (sincerely), "Never mind, I forgive you." Later, John finds himself in a difficult situation and turns to Mary for help. Mary, still harboring resentment over the earlier incident, responds, "Why should I help you after what you did to me?" John then reminds her, "But you already forgave me for that."[10] At this point, Mary could respond by saying, "Well, I guess I really didn't." But she could also respond by saying, "Yes, you're right" and proceed to help him.

In the view that construes "I forgive you" as a report of how one feels—reporting the fact that one has overcome one's resentment—only the first response is open to Mary. Otherwise, it would be contradictory of Mary to maintain that she forgave John while continuing to harbor resentment against him. (Of course, we might indict Mary on lesser charges of being ambivalent or self-deceiving.) Thus, at the risk of logical confusion, her only response would be to declare that she had not forgiven him, after all. However, in the view that construes "I forgive you" as an expression of how one feels, the fact that Mary continues to harbor resentment does not undermine her having forgiven John at all.

The argument could be made that Mary did not succeed in expressing her forgiveness when injured by John, as evidenced by the fact of her later resentment. However, this argument would have validity only if, at the time Mary said "I forgive you," feelings of resentment festered within her. But if Mary was sincere when she uttered the words, her later resentment would not at all undermine her earlier success in expressing her attitude. To see this more clearly, consider the locution "I welcome you," said (sincerely) by a host to an arriving party guest. Suppose that, following the guest's entrance into the house, the host treats the guest as an intruder (perhaps because the host suddenly learns of some fact about the guest of which he disapproves). If the host was sincere when he said "I welcome you," the fact that he subsequently treats the guest as an intruder does not undermine his earlier success in expressing his attitude.

Furthermore, quite apart from how Mary feels, if we look at what she says from the perspective of John, there is no reason to doubt that what she says is sincere. Clearly, in the absence of evidence to the contrary at the time (Mary's fingers are crossed or she is talking tongue-in-cheek), John has no reason to doubt that Mary succeeds in expressing her attitude when she utters the words in question. Thus, just as the guest has no reason to doubt that the host is sincere when he tells him "I welcome you," John has no reason to doubt that Mary is sincere when she tells him "I forgive you." From the listener's perspective, the claim holds so long as there is no evidence to the contrary. Thus, Mary's second response is intuitively plausible, and it is on this intuitive plausibility that I ground my position.

Still, it is important to ascertain what it is that accounts for this plausibility. Certainly, it cannot be the *meaning* of forgiveness since, on the models we have examined, it would turn out that Mary did not succeed in forgiving John—which would be no help to us here. What will help is if we ask what it was that Mary was *doing* when she said to John, "I forgive you." As I see it, what Mary was doing was *expressing an attitude*. Since to express an attitude is to perform an act, it follows that "I forgive you" is a performative utterance or—what amounts to the same thing—a "speech act."[11]

Of course, saying that forgiveness is an attitude that gets expressed in the locution "I forgive you" is not to say fully what forgiveness is. We must still characterize the attitude. Let us assume that an attitude cannot be characterized without referring to the judgments on which it is founded.[12] We may then state, quite confidently, that it is precisely such judgments that a speaker represents in expressing forgiveness. What these judgments are will be examined below.

The Presuppositions of Forgiveness

In expressing his forgiveness of an agent X for his act A, a speaker S represents as true the following statements:

(1) X did A;
(2) A was wrong; and
(3) X was responsible for doing A.[13]

There are two points to be made with respect to (1). First, there can be no question of forgiveness unless A was committed by a moral agent. As H. J. N. Horsbrugh correctly states, "One cannot forgive a rock for falling on one's foot or a cougar for attacking one's child, even though a child might kick the rock and the father might shoot the cougar."[14] Where X is a minor, the question of forgiveness arises only for those actions for which minors are responsible (getting in the Jello, writing on the walls, etc.—see (3)). Second, it must indeed be X who committed A. To forgive X for having committed A when it was actually Y who committed it would be an error on the part of S. So, too, to forgive X for having committed A when it was actually B that he did (provided B was not wrong—see (2)) would also be an error on the part of S. So, for forgiveness to occur (as opposed to the false belief that it has occurred), the person who is forgiven must be the one who in fact committed the act in question.

Statements (2) and (3) are a bit more complicated. Certainly, forgiveness presupposes moral wrongdoing.[15] Were this not the case, there would be nothing to forgive. True, we sometimes say we forgive even in the absence of moral wrongdoing. Where, for example, our partner in bridge makes a foolish move that results in our losing the game, we may say we forgive him, though the wrong he committed was not a moral one. However, use of the term in such cases is, strictly speaking, idiosyncratic. Otherwise, forgiveness would collapse into *justification* or *excuse*[16] and would lack a domain it could call its own.

To see this, consider the concepts of justification and excuse. To justify an action that appears to be a wrongdoing is to say that it was prima facie wrong but, because of other morally relevant factors (e.g., the need to save a life), on balance the action was the right thing to do. At least this is Austin's account of justification: To justify an action is "to accept responsibility but deny that it was bad."[17] To excuse is to say that what was done was morally wrong but, because of certain factors about the agent (e.g., he was insane), it would be unfair to hold the agent responsible or blame him for the wrong action. Again quoting Austin, in offering an excuse "we admit that [what we did] was bad but don't accept full, or even any, responsibility."[18]

Returning, then, to declarations of forgiveness for wrongs committed other than moral ones, we can easily see how they must be considered idiosyncratic, at least from the perspective of standard usage. Having made a foolish move, our partner in bridge can be excused for his action provided the harm was not ill intended. In other words, if we realize that our partner thought he was doing good, then the harm brought about can be said to have been a mistake. He really should be excused rather than forgiven. On the other hand, if the harm that he caused was ill intended—that is, designed to cause us to lose the game—then, because of his intentions, his action can be classified as morally wrong, which makes our forgiving him a standard case.

In saying that such declarations of forgiveness are idiosyncratic, I am not implying that this usage is entirely foreign to the standard "I forgive you." There is, I believe, a family likeness between the two. Nevertheless, as I mentioned in Chapter 1, this likeness still leaves room for the development of a paradigm,[19] and the paradigm case for the use of "forgiveness" is where the wrong inflicted is a distinctly moral one.[20]

But if statements (1) through (3) are necessary for forgiveness to occur, they are not, by themselves, sufficient. I cannot, for instance, forgive Meletus for prosecuting Socrates—not because what Meletus did was not wrong, but because I have not been injured by his behavior. Forgiveness is primarily a personal response to injury. Whether it is *essentially* a personal response to injury is a question taken up later in the chapter.[21] For now, suffice it to say that, in addition to representing statements (1) through (3), S also represents that

(4) S was personally injured by X's doing A.

However, statements (1) through (4) are not sufficient for forgiveness to occur, either. Not only must a person be personally injured by another's wrongdoing; that person must also take offense or resent the wrongdoer's behavior. That is, the injured person must hold it against the wrongdoer. While resenting personal injuries is only natural, it is not, as we shall see, inevitable. For this reason, we must add still another statement:

(5) S resented being injured by X's doing A.

What is now needed is an analysis of the concepts of injury and resentment, which are paramount to understanding the forgiving response.

Moral Injury

By "injury" as it is used in statement (4), I specifically mean *moral* injury. This follows from statements (1) through (3). Colloquially, we use the term "injury" to refer to all harm, irrespective of origin. We speak, for instance, of injuries received from bee stings, boating accidents, and ski mishaps, but we also speak of injuries resulting from insults, embarrassments, and attacks on our pride. The difference between the first class of examples and the second is that the first class is caused by something other than moral agents, while the second class is caused specifically by moral agents. It is the latter that is properly termed "moral injury," and here I shall reserve the term "injury" to refer to a given harm that is or was somebody's fault.

This distinguishing between moral and nonmoral injury is not unique. According to Strawson, for an injury to have occurred (in the moral sense), there must be some expression of ill-will (or lack of good-will) toward the injured person.[22] And W. D. Ross, who listed what he thought were the main prima facie obligations, included the duty not to cause injury as one of them.[23] Commenting on Ross's listing of this duty and apparent neglect of the duty not to kill, R. B. Brandt notes that Ross might have thought that killing a human being is sometimes not an injury (in the moral sense) and that it is a prima facie duty not to kill only when the killing constitutes an injury.[24] This analysis of what constitutes an injury sheds further light on Horsbrugh's comment that one cannot forgive a rock for falling on one's foot or a cougar for attacking one's child. We may now say that forgiveness is inapplicable to these situations not only because rocks and cougars are not moral agents, but because they cannot cause injuries in the relevant sense.

Resentment

Having defined "injury," I turn to the concept of resentment, which naturally is occasioned by injury.[25] By "resentment," I mean the anger that one might properly feel at having been personally injured.[26] So defined, resentment has a "desert basis"[27] that constitutes an essential part of it, and it is this that distinguishes it from anger per se.

In saying that resentment contains a desert basis in a way that anger does not, I am presupposing that emotions are in some sense rational. In this, I am going against the received view of the emotions, according to which emotions are visceral passions—that is, states that merely happen to us, along the same lines as sensations. Pascal, for one, held this view when he said that "Man's war within [is] between his Reason and his Passions,"[28] and the view finds expression in such common phrases as "I couldn't help it; I was angry" and "She's not responsible; she's in love."[29]

There is, however, an alternative school of thought, according to which emotions involve beliefs as well as sensations. Representative of this school are such people as Bernard Williams,[30] William Lyons,[31] and P. F. Strawson.[32] In their view, emotions involve specific attitudes and certain ways of looking at the world. If, for instance, we say that someone overreacted to a situation or blew some event out of proportion, we tacitly suggest that some reactions could have been proper in proportion to the provocation of the situation. In this sense, my discussion of resentment assumes a cognitivist theory of the emotions. That is, it makes some aspect of thought central to the definition of the emotion itself. I assume that the emotions involve certain evaluative beliefs that accompany physiological changes in the person who experiences them.

In distinguishing between anger and resentment, I am essentially following Bishop Joseph Butler, who maintains that "they are essentially distinguished in this, that the latter [i.e., resentment] is never occasioned by harm, distinct from injury; and its natural proper end is to remedy or prevent only that harm, which implies, or is supposed to imply, injury or moral wrong."[33] And again:

> *Sudden anger*, upon certain occasions, is mere instinct: as merely so, as the disposition to close our eyes upon the apprehension of somewhat

> falling into them; and no more necessarily implies any degree of reason. I say, *necessarily*: for to be sure *hasty*, as well as *deliberate*, anger may be occasioned by injury or contempt; in which case reason suggests to our thoughts that injury and contempt, which is the occasion of the passion: but I am speaking of the former only so far as it is to be distinguished from the latter. The only way in which our reason and understanding can raise anger, is by representing to our mind injustice or injury of some kind or other. Now momentary anger is frequently raised, not only without any real, but without any apparent reason; that is, without any appearance of injury, as distinct from hurt or pain.[34]

Butler is not alone in construing resentment along these lines. According to Strawson, occasions for resentment are "situations in which one person is offended or injured by the action of another and in which—in the absence of special considerations—the offended person might naturally or normally be expected to feel resentment."[35] Jean Hampton offers this definition: "Resentment is an emotion which reflects [our] judgment that the harmful treatment [we] experienced should not have been intentionally inflicted on [us] by [our] assailants insofar as it is *not* appropriate given [our] value and rank."[36] According to Andrew von Hirsch and Nils Jareborg, resentment refers to those situations when "*the actor acts in anger at his victim, and has good reason for being angry in virtue of some wrong or impropriety suffered at his victim's hands*."[37] And finally, Joel Feinberg says, "To resent someone . . . is not merely to dislike him, but to have a negative feeling toward him in virtue of something he has done, and what follows the 'in virtue of' is as much a part of the feeling as its unfriendly or aggressive character."[38]

So, resentment is the emotion that reflects the belief that the injury received should not have been intentionally inflicted in the manner done. It is a form of personal protest, which, in the words of Jeffrie Murphy, "expresses our respect for self, for others, and for morality."[39] And while the term "resentment" is rather archaic, what it refers to is familiar enough. Consider, for example, a case where my competitor gets something I wanted for myself. I may be angry at him, but I have no justification for my anger. However, if my competitor has lied or cheated me out of something that is rightfully mine, I have justification for my anger, and it is this kind of anger that is properly termed "resentment." This is the term's original, moral significance; the Oxford English Dictionary defines it as "a strong feeling of ill-will or anger against the author of a wrong or affront." The logic of resentment is such that it is not only *occasioned* by the behavior of the person at whom it is directed, but it is *warranted* by that behavior as well. Thus, to again quote Feinberg, "we do not use such words as 'resent' . . . unless there is an ostensible desert basis of the logically appropriate sort for our feeling. . . . We can feel hostility for no apparent reason, but we cannot resent someone for 'no reason at all.' "[40] F. H. Bradley once wrote, in a famous line, that punishment without desert is not punishment.[41] In a similar vein, we can say that resentment without desert is not resentment.

That resentment is an eminently *personal* response to injury is a thesis also shared by many of these theorists. Citing favorably from Webster's, Feinberg maintains that resentment "is largely confined to responses to *personal* injury and affront."[42] Von Hirsch and Jareborg argue that, while "all sorts of things V does might exasperate A, and some things V does might infuriate A, . . . what is crucial [to A's feeling resentment] is his having a *good reason* for his anger, *stemming from some misdeed committed by the victim against him*."[43] What follows from this is that one can resent only what is an injury to oneself (or someone to whom one is closely related).[44] Thus, although there may be much to be angry about when learning of an injury to another, such anger lies outside the arena of resentment. Murphy refers to such third-party anger as "indignation," as does Martin Golding, who writes that "Smith may be resentful towards me, and his attitude would be one of *justified resentment*; outside parties, on the other hand, may be indignant over the matter, and their attitude would be one of *justified indignation*."[45]

In construing resentment as a response to injury, it is important not to confuse it with the concept of blame. Like resentment, blame involves our holding an action against someone. However, unlike resentment, in blaming a person, we make no representation that we have been angered in any way.[46] To see this more clearly, consider the fact that a person is blameworthy even when there is no one to blame him, but a person is not resented if the one he injured does not resent him.[47] A person is "to blame" if that person is accountable, answerable, or otherwise liable for the wrong he committed. "If," though, as Feinberg writes, "we mean by 'blame' any outwardly manifested disapproval of a person for his defective performance, then the relations between blaming and 'being to blame' are diverse and complex."[48] As I am using the term, "blame" is a supervenient property that attaches to one who is morally responsible for the wrong he has committed. Because of this, we must not take forgiveness to be opposed to blame. L. C. Holborow, for one, is mistaken when he writes that "the respect in which forgiveness represents a refusal to *hold* the faulty action *against* the player brings into clearer focus what is involved in blaming him."[49] If forgiveness were directed toward blame, as Holborow seems to think, then it would follow that, after being forgiven, the wrongdoer would no longer be morally to blame. No one has the power to bring this about.

If resentment is anger that one might properly feel on having been personally injured, it is not inevitable that one will feel it. To a great extent, resentment presupposes a certain measure of self-respect. Murphy explains,

> One reason we so deeply resent moral injuries done to us is simply that they hurt us in some tangible or sensible way; it is because such injuries are also *messages*, i.e., symbolic communications. They are ways a wrongdoer has of saying to us "I count and you do not," "I can use you for my purposes," or "I am up high and you are down below."[50]

But we can, of course, acquiesce to the injury, believing that we are unworthy of more dignified treatment. We might be so laden with neurotic guilt as to think we deserve bad treatment. To use Thomas Hill's examples, we can be like the "Uncle Tom" who does not resent less qualified whites when they take over his job, or the "Deferential Wife" who does not resent her abusive husband.[51] In both these cases, the victims of injuries do not feel resentment because they have too little self-respect.

At the other extreme, we can have too much self-respect and believe we are worthy of so much better treatment that to feel resentment would be beneath us. A prince who is mistaken for a pauper and who fails to receive royal treatment may feel no resentment by simple virtue of his nobility.[52] Such would be the Nietzschean view, according to which a truly strong person does not feel resentment, because other people cannot hurt him; in that sense, they simply do not matter. Just as we do not resent insects when they happen to sting us, so too we should not resent injuries by people who are beneath us.[53] This may explain why Socrates, for instance, did not resent his persecutors; he may have held himself in so high a regard as to be beyond resenting what injuries he received.[54]

The question of whether one *should* feel resentment for injuries received is a separate question and will be addressed in Chapter 4. For now, suffice it to say that however natural it is to resent an injury, it is not inevitable that one will do so. However, the question of forgiveness does not arise unless resentment is in fact present. P. Twambley has written, "To put things in a somewhat [Anthony] Kenny-an manner, one can only forgive what one could resent."[55] We need only notice that forgiveness requires moral wrongdoing; without it, as has been said earlier, there would be nothing to forgive. However, in forgiving a person, we cannot make the wrongdoer no longer to blame; no one has this power. But if forgiveness requires wrongdoing and does not operate to eliminate blame, to what then is it directed? The answer is that it is directed at the resentment occasioned by the injury. That it is not directed at wrongdoing per se and that it is not directed at injury simpliciter has, I think, been sufficiently demonstrated.

Interestingly enough, Norvin Richards has recently taken issue with the claim that forgiveness presupposes resentment at all.[56] Responding to the claim that forgiveness is the overcoming of resentment, it is Richards's contention that one could forgive in the absence of resentment so long as there exists any kind of negative feeling, such as contempt, sadness, disappointment, and so on.[57] However, what Richards overlooks is that resentment is linked to self-respect in a way that other feelings are not. If, as I shall argue later in this chapter, only the injured party has the right to forgive, this is because it is the one who has been injured whose self-respect is exposed. This is why I cannot forgive Meletus for having prosecuted Socrates, though I feel sadness and disappointment over what he did.

We see then that, in expressing his forgiveness, S must have resented being injured by X's act. Still, there is yet a further statement that S represents:

(6) S has overcome his resentment for X's doing A, or is at least willing to try to overcome it.

Now, for several reasons, this is the trickiest presupposition. First, as we have already seen, there is a formidable tradition that *defines* forgiveness as the overcoming of resentment. However, we have also seen that defining forgiveness in this manner leads to some vexing problems that we can avoid only if we maintain that a speaker *presupposes* this statement in expressing forgiveness—or so I shall argue. Second, unlike statements (1) through (5), which S also presupposes in expressing forgiveness, it is not at all clear that the truth of (6) is required for forgiveness to occur—at least in the same way that the truth of the others is required. As I shall argue in the next section, if S "offends" against (1) through (5), then we can say with Austin that the forgiveness has "misfired." However, if S offends against (6), then—rather than misfiring—it may be that S has incurred an "infelicity" of another sort. But since I deal with these issues further in this chapter, I shall resist a discussion of statement (6) and simply note its presence for now.

We may thus sum up and say that, in expressing forgiveness of an agent X for his act A, a speaker S represents as true all of the following:

(1) X did A;
(2) A was wrong;
(3) X was responsible for doing A;
(4) S was personally injured by X's doing A;
(5) S resented being injured by X's doing A; and
(6) S has overcome his resentment for X's doing A, or is at least willing to try to overcome it.

"I Forgive You" as a Performative Utterance

In claiming that "I forgive you" is a performative utterance, I am not implying that the only way to forgive an individual is to utter the verbal formula. As Austin explains, to issue a performative utterance "*is* to perform an action—an action, perhaps, which one could scarcely perform, at least with so much precision, in any other way."[58] Consider, for instance, the locution "I do take this woman to be my lawful wedded wife," said by a bridegroom to his bride before the altar. In saying this, the bridegroom performs the act of getting married. But this is not the only way to get married. One could, for instance, get married under common law by living with someone for a number of years. So, too, one could forgive another by having the requisite attitude, independent of any verbal expression. But if "I forgive you" does, as I have urged, pin down the essential way in which one expresses the attitude of forgiveness—that is, shows that the speaker regards the object of forgiveness in a certain light—then the way to perform the act of forgiveness "with so much precision" is simply to utter the verbal formula.

For the forgiveness to "take effect," however, one must forgive under "appropriate circumstances." Just as the performative utterance "to bet" is not, as Austin explains, simply to utter the words "I bet" but to do so before the race is over, with money in hand, and so forth,[59] so, too, to express forgiveness is not merely to utter the words "I forgive you" but to do so under appropriate circumstances. Once again, there are statements that the speaker must represent as true, or, in William Alston's useful phrase, "take responsibility for holding."[60]

Austin's Six Conditions

Austin lists six conditions that must be satisfied for locutions in general to count as performative utterances:

1. There must exist an accepted conventional procedure having a certain conventional effect, that procedure to include the uttering of certain words by certain persons in certain circumstances;
2. The particular persons and circumstances in a given case must be appropriate for the invocation of the particular procedure invoked;
3. The procedure must be executed by all participants correctly and
4. Completely;
5. Where, as often, the procedure is designed for use by persons having certain thoughts or feelings or for the inauguration of certain consequential conduct on the part of the participant, then a person participating in and so invoking the procedure must in fact have these thoughts or feelings, and the participant must intend so to conduct themselves; and further
6. Must actually so conduct themselves subsequently.[61]

It is worthwhile to consider the import of these conditions before examining the way they pertain to "I forgive you."

The first thing to notice is that, if we offend against any of the first four conditions, then, according to Austin, the act in question is not achieved. Consider, for instance, the expression "I now pronounce you husband and wife," said at the altar by the justice of the peace to a couple about to get married. If the formula is uttered incorrectly (violating the third condition above) or the couple is not in a position to get married because they are already married to others (violating the second condition), or it is the caterer rather than the justice of the peace who is conducting the ceremony (again, violating the second condition above), then the act in question—that is, marrying—is not successfully performed. Because of these so-called infelicities, the act is aborted, and the locution "misfires."[62] Thus, the claim that a certain kind of sentence is a performative utterance is a defeasible one, which is to say that the claim holds until it is defeated. What defeats the pronunciation of marriage in the example cited is the existence of just those infelicitous circumstances of which mention was made.

In contrast to the first four conditions, the fifth and sixth conditions are such that, if offended against, the act in question *is* achieved but, as Austin says, the formula is "abused."[63] The act is, as he puts it, "hollow," "empty," and does not characteristically "take effect." However—and this is the main point—unlike offenses against the first four conditions, a violation of these latter two does not render the act void and without effect. To illustrate, consider the formula "I promise to do thus-and-such." If the formula is uttered without offending against any of the first four conditions, then a promise has been made, notwithstanding subsequent developments such as that the promise is not fulfilled, which is an offense against the sixth condition.

In sum, performative utterances are subject to two kinds of failure. They can either misfire, in which case the act in question is not successfully performed, or they can be abused, in which case the act in question is performed but the act is hollow or empty. It is of the utmost importance to note that infelicities are failures of performative utterances in a different dimension from that of falsity, and the reason for this is that performative utterances are not, strictly speaking, true or false. Truth and falsity are properties of *statements*, and performative utterances are not statements. Thus, when the bridegroom says during the marriage ceremony, "I do take this woman to be my lawful wedded wife," he is not reporting that he is getting married (which report *would be* either true or false); rather, he is performing the act of getting married.

However, to say that performative utterances are neither true nor false is not to deny that they *imply* statements that are true or false. Ordinarily, we talk of statements implying other statements. Thus if S_1 implies S_2, then it is impossible for S_2 to be false if S_1 is true. But this is only one of the senses of the word "implies." In quite a different sense—first pointed out by G. E. Moore—my saying "the cat is on the mat" implies that I believe it to be so. However, unlike strict logical implication, if I do not believe that the cat is on the mat, it does not follow that the cat is not on the mat.[64] It is this restricted sense of "implies" to which Austin appeals in saying that performative utterances imply statements that are either true or false. Strictly speaking, it is the person and not the statement that is doing the implying.

Still, there is more to the matter than this. For some statements that are implied by performative utterances, their falsity results in the performative's misfiring. For other statements, their falsity results in the performative's abuse. Consider, for instance, the case where the bridegroom says, "I do take this woman to my lawful wedded wife," implying, as he says so, that he is not already married with wife living, sane, undivorced, and so forth.[65] Suppose further that what he implies is false: That is, he is already married to another woman. In this case, the bridegroom has only gone through the motions of getting married; he has not, however, succeeded in getting married. In contrast, consider the case where Jones says to Smith, "I congratulate you for having been promoted to executive officer," implying, as he says so, that Smith deserves the promotion, has worked hard for it, and so forth. Suppose here that what Jones implies is false: That is, Smith does not deserve the promotion, has in fact not worked hard for it, and so forth. In this case, Jones *has* succeeded in congratulating Smith, though he had no business doing so. Thus, the truth of what we imply when we issue a performative utterance can affect the very performance of the speech act, with the result that the act does not take place if its implied statements are not true. On the other hand, while the falsity of certain other implied statements may not affect the performance of the act, it can result in an abuse of a specified kind.

Having outlined the general picture of performative utterances, we can now determine the precise extent to which "I forgive you" falls within its scope.[66] With respect to the first condition, we have already seen (very early in the chapter) that "I forgive you" is an accepted conventional procedure that we use to forgive. Austin's example of a procedure that would not be conventionally accepted is the utterance of "I divorce you," said to a wife in a Catholic country where divorce is illegal.[67] Since no such problems arise with respect to "I forgive you," this condition needs no further elaboration.

When it comes to the second condition, the matter is more complicated. From what has been said thus far, it would seem that, for particular persons and circumstances to be "appropriate" for the invocation of the procedure, certain conditions must obtain. Specifically, in expressing forgiveness, S must represent that X did A, A was wrong, X was responsible for doing A, S was injured by X's doing A, and S resented being injured by X's doing A. Now if for any reason it should turn out that any of these statements is *false*, then the forgiveness would misfire, and the act would not take effect. S's saying "I forgive you" in the absence of the truth of these statements is rather like performing a baptism on a penguin. As Austin puts it, when performing a baptism, the one performing represents that the one baptized is susceptible of that exploit. However, since penguins are not susceptible to that exploit, one's saying "I baptize you" in their regard would be null and void. The most we can say is that the person who does so has gone through the form of baptism but has not succeeded in baptizing in fact.[68] This follows from the first kind of failure to which performative utterances are subject.

Austin's Second Condition and Third-party Forgiveness

At this point, we should pause to consider whether "I forgive you" misfires when the speaker is someone other than the one who was injured by X's misconduct. Ostensibly, for particular persons to be appropriate for the invocation of the procedure, they must have standing both to forgive and be forgiven. In other words, since it is a presupposition of forgiveness that it be given by the person who has been personally injured, it would appear that only the victim of an injury is in a position to forgive, and only his wrongdoer is in a position to be forgiven. Stated otherwise, for S to express forgiveness of X, it must indeed be S who was the victim of the injury. And if X did not injure S (either because there was in fact no injury or because it was someone other than S who was injured), then S's saying "I forgive you" misfires, and the forgiveness is null and void.

The question of whether "I forgive you" misfires when uttered by someone other than the victim of an injury was poignantly raised by Dostoyevsky in *The Brothers Karamazov*. Ivan Karamazov tells the story of an aristocratic general who has his dogs kill a peasant boy for injuring the paw of the general's favorite hound. Ivan is outraged at the thought that anyone except the boy could forgive the general for the peasant boy's death.[69] In considering whether the boy's mother could forgive on behalf of her dead child, Ivan has this to say:

> I don't want the mother to embrace the oppressor who threw her son to the dogs. She dare not forgive him. Let her forgive him for herself, if she will. Let her forgive the torturer for the immeasurable suffering of her mother's heart. But the sufferings of her tortured child she has no right to forgive; she dare not forgive the torturer, even if the child were to forgive him.[70]

Simon Wiesenthal poses the same question in an equally poignant way when, in *The Sunflower*, he writes of a chilling experience he had while serving in a work-crew of Jewish concentration camp inmates.

The work-crew is taken to a German military hospital in Poland, at which time a nurse leads Wiesenthal to a dying SS soldier who tells him of his participation in an event that led to the murder of some 300 Jews.

> "I know that what I have told you is terrible," says the soldier. "In the long nights that I have been waiting for my death, time and time again I have longed to talk about it to a Jew and beg forgiveness from him. Only I didn't know whether there were any Jews left."[71]

Wiesenthal goes on to relate how he did not forgive the SS soldier and how this incident later challenged his heart and soul. "Was my silence at the bedside of the dying Nazi right or wrong?" he asks. While Wiesenthal here is raising the moral question of whether he ought to have forgiven the soldier, many of the respondents to whom he posed this question maintained that Wiesenthal could not have forgiven him because, as one put it (quoting Dryden), "forgiveness, to the injured doth belong."[72] Abraham Heschel said, "No one can forgive crimes committed by other people . . . even God Himself can only forgive sins committed against Himself, not against man."[73] Terrence Prittie, echoing these sentiments, argued, "A persecuted Jew could only forgive wrongs done to him personally; he could not possibly forgive genocide."[74]

So the question remains: Does "I forgive you" misfire when directed at a wrongdoer who is not one's injurer? Can S express his forgiveness of X for A when A has injured someone other than S? As Horsbrugh sees it, there are two classes of cases that must be distinguished when considering the question of third-party forgiveness. The first class of cases concerns instances when S uses the term "to forgive" when commenting on injuries inflicted on a person or group of persons *not* intimately associated with S. "Such uses of the verb 'to forgive,' " writes Horsbrugh, "are almost invariably negative in the sense that [S] asserts that he is unable or unwilling to forgive the person or group of persons responsible for the injury."[75] The second class of cases concerns instances in which S uses the term "to forgive" when commenting on injuries inflicted on a person or group of persons with which S *is* intimately associated.

Illustrative of the first class of cases is S's refusal to express his forgiveness of the Nazis for what they did to the Jews where S himself is not Jewish. As Horsbrugh sees it, cases of this kind can be interpreted in any of three ways. First, when S says he is unwilling to forgive the Nazis, what he means may be that he is not prepared to overlook what they did to the Jews. Understood this way, S's saying "I can't forgive the Nazis" does not imply that he could forgive them if his sentiments were other than what they are. Rather, he is to be understood as saying that the Nazis ought not to be forgiven by any one or another of the various persons (or groups of persons) who may have the standing to do so. In this sense, the word "unforgivable" shares a logic similar to that of "undesirable," which means not that the object of desire is not desired—as Mill perhaps believed[76]—but that the object in question ought not to be desired.[77] Thus, "forgiveness" here is put to an idiosyncratic use.

Second, what S means when he says that he is unwilling to express his forgiveness of the Nazis may be that he is identifying himself with the Jewish victims, thereby claiming that he too suffered an injury at their hands. Here, "forgiveness" appears to be used in a nonidiosyncratic way. However, it is Horsbrugh's view that, if this is what S means, then he is misusing the language of forgiveness, since he is not entitled to attach himself to the ranks of the injured as he is neither a Jew himself nor a relative or close friend of any of their victims.[78]

Third, what S means when he says he is unwilling to express his forgiveness of the Nazis may be that he is responding to their victims' suffering simply as a fellow member of the human race. He is sympathizing—as in John Donne's observation: "Any man's death diminishes me, because I am involved in Mankind." Baron von Hugel once wrote that "souls—all human souls—are deeply interconnected."[79] And this does seem to express a lofty ideal. However, such a claim, even if true, trivializes forgiveness. And in any case, it is—as Horsbrugh rightfully points out—unacceptable when applied to our example, for the spirit of Donne's remark (and that of von Hugel's) does not take sides between the Nazis and their victims.[80] It is too inclusive and proclaims a brotherhood embracing both sinner and saint.

Illustrative of the second class of third-party cases is S's refusal to express forgiveness of X for an injury that X inflicted on S's daughter, D. Unlike the first class, cases such as this are genuine cases of forgiveness, evidenced by the fact that, whereas X may plead with S to be forgiven for what he did to D, there is no question of any ex-Nazi—however repentant—asking S to forgive him for what he did to the Jews.[81] According to Horsbrugh, what accounts for this difference is the fact that, in these and like cases, there is a personal relationship, which makes it inevitable that someone other than the immediate victim sustains a moral injury. In this particular case, there is the relationship between S and D, between S and X, and between D and X. The relationship between S and D makes it virtually certain that, when D is injured, S is injured as well. What this suggests, according to Horsbrugh, is that X really is pleading with S to be forgiven for the injury he inflicted on S. Thus, unlike the first class of cases, the second turns out, on analysis, to be a nonidiosyncratic use of "forgiveness," after all, despite the form of the words employed.[82]

Horsbrugh's classification of cases into those where third-party forgiveness turns out not to be forgiveness at all and those that turn out to be run-of-the-mill forgiveness is essentially correct. His analysis has the virtue of preserving our intuition that "forgiveness, to the injured doth belong," as well as the virtue of leaving the presuppositions of forgiveness intact. It also preserves our intuitive stigmatizing of those who would forgive wrongdoers when they themselves have not been injured. This stigmatization is captured by our declaring that such individuals "have no right to forgive." However, Horsbrugh's distinction remains arbitrary in the absence of an argument showing why it is that, just because I have no personal relationship with one who has been injured, I cannot feel resentment and consequently forgive. To put the matter another way, while it *may* be presumptuous of me to forgive one who has injured someone other than myself, it is not at all clear that it *must* be presumptuous. I can, for instance, psychologically identify with those whom I do not know personally.

William Neblett, for one, has challenged the belief that only the injured party has a right to forgive.

> Suppose, for example, that an individual A harms another individual B, and as a consequence a third party C, who is close to B, is also indirectly harmed. If B now wishes to forgive A, his "right" to do so might well be challenged by C. Even if B tells A that he forgives him, C may still challenge this by saying to A, "*I* do not forgive you, and no matter what B says or does, you are not forgiven." This example not only illustrates problems with the "right to forgive," but it also reveals the complexities involved in the relationship between (1) "forgiving someone" and (2) "being forgiven."[83]

Neblett is correct as far as he goes, but he does not go far enough. What we are interested in knowing is not whether some individual C who is close to B has the right to forgive the wrongdoer A. This much has already been granted. What we want to know now is whether an individual Z *who is not close to B* can forgive A for the wrong he has done. Again, we need an argument showing that having a personal relationship with a victim is somehow relevant to the right to forgive.

Can such an argument be made? Is there any reason to believe that an injury to one with whom I have no personal relationship is different, in relevant respects, from an injury to one with whom I have this relationship? Previously, we have drawn a distinction between *resentment* on the one hand and *indignation* on the other and suggested that forgiveness is possible where resentment is present, as opposed to indignation.[84] If we attend to the difference between these emotions, the argument we are seeking will begin to emerge.[85]

Following Murphy, I have urged that resentment is a form of personal protest that expresses our regard for self, for others, and for the normative order. Indignation, on the other hand (or "resentment on behalf of another," as Strawson puts it),[86] is a form of personal protest that expresses our respect not for the self, but rather for others and the normative order only. Thus, the essential difference between resentment and indignation is that the former is tied up with self-respect, while the latter is not. What follows from this is that, when I am personally injured and resent the injury, I do so because, inter alia, my self-respect is on the line. However, my self-respect is *not* on the line when I am indignant over injuries inflicted on strangers. Consequently, to the extent that "I forgive you" presupposes that I resent you, I can only forgive what is an injury to myself or others with whom I psychologically identify. This follows analytically.

Of course, the validity of this argument hinges on the legitimacy of distinguishing resentment and indignation in the manner specified. It is my contention that the difference mentioned is not arbitrary, but does reflect the essence of the emotions involved. Certainly, the distinction I am pointing to is the canonical one. In addition to Murphy, Strawson maintains that—unlike resentment—in cases of indignation, "one's own interest and dignity are not involved."[87] Jean Hampton has this to say about the two emotions:

> Indignation is the emotional protest against immoral treatment whose object is the defense of the value which this action violated, whereas resentment is an emotion whose object is the defiant reaffirmation of one's rank and value in the face of treatment calling them into question.[88]

So one cannot forgive what is an injury to a stranger because one cannot resent such an injury, resentment being linked with self-respect. Previously, we said that third parties lack "standing" to forgive vicariously, and the use of this term was not incidental. The concept of standing is a legal one and focuses on the question of whether the litigant is the proper party to bring a lawsuit, rather than on the question of whether the issue is justiciable. Analogously, the question of third-party forgiveness is not simply a question of whether the injury in question is one that could be brought before a moral tribunal. The question is whether a person who has not been injured is the proper party to bring it. Since, as I have urged, only the injured party has standing to forgive (he alone being the one who could feel resentment), it follows that third-party forgiveness cannot be tendered.

Finally, there is yet another reason why third-party forgiveness is conceptually troublesome. There is a sense in which the recipient of third-party forgiveness cannot survive the "publicity" criterion of being forgiven. Unless I am mistaken, what the wrongdoer wants in seeking forgiveness is forgiveness *from the one he has injured*. Without forgiveness from the victim of the injury, the wrongdoer cannot see himself as forgiven. This is true even if third parties have said they have forgiven him. Conversely, if the victim of an injury has tendered his forgiveness, then—notwithstanding what third parties have said or done—the wrongdoer can see himself as forgiven.

In sum, "I forgive you" misfires when uttered by one not personally injured (or by one not related to the one who was injured). What follows from this—contra Ivan Karamazov—is that the peasant boy's mother *can* forgive the general whose dogs killed her son. This is because the relationship between mother and son is such that an injury to the son is an injury to the mother, so that the mother's forgiveness is really for her own injury. On the other hand, Prince Myshkin of Dostoyevsky's *The Idiot* presumably could not forgive the general, since his reaction to the event would (no doubt) be one of indignation.[89] Whether Wiesenthal could forgive the Nazi depends on what relationship existed between himself and those whom the Nazi had murdered. If there was the type of relationship that made an injury to other Jews an injury to Wiesenthal, then—since he could have felt resentment—he could have forgiven. However, he could not have forgiven him for the crime of genocide without putting "forgiveness" to an eccentric use.

The Last Four Conditions and Their Infelicities

Returning, then, to Austin's conditions, the third and fourth are self-explanatory. If, as Austin points out, I say, "I open this library," but the key snaps in the lock, then the act of opening the library is aborted and the formula misfires.[90] Similarly, if the victim of an injury (or, as we may now say, one who psychologically identifies with the victim) chokes on the words "I forgive you"—perhaps because he still harbors resentment—his expression of forgiveness will be abortive and ineffective. These are examples of how a performative utterance can misfire by failing to satisfy the third and fourth conditions. Of greater interest for the present analysis are the fifth and sixth conditions, which, as we have seen, are abuses of performatives but do not prevent the act from taking effect.

With respect to the fifth condition, Austin maintains that we abuse a formula if, for example, we utter it insincerely. "If I say 'I promise to . . . ' without in the least intending to carry out the promised action, perhaps not even believing that it is in my power to carry it out, the promise is hollow. It is made, certainly; but still, there is an 'unhappiness': I have *abused* the formula."[91]

With respect to the sixth condition, Austin says,

> Let us suppose that our act has been performed: everything has gone off quite normally, and also, if you like, sincerely. In that case the performative utterance will characteristically "take effect." We do not mean by that that such-and-such a future event is or will be brought about as an effect of this action functioning as a cause. We mean rather that, in consequence of the performance of this act, such-and-such a future event, *if* it happens, will be *in order*. . . . If I have said "I promise," I shall not be in order if I break my word; if I have said "I welcome you," I shall not be in order if I proceed to treat you as an enemy or intruder. Thus we say that, even when the performative has taken effect, there may always crop up a third kind of unhappiness, which we call "breach of commitment."[92]

So, where the performative utterance is intended for use by persons having certain thoughts or feelings or for the inauguration of certain consequential conduct, S must in fact have these thoughts or feelings, intend to conduct himself accordingly, and actually do so. However, to emphasize once more, failure to satisfy these conditions does not prevent the act from taking place; the act takes place despite the infelicity.

The Conditions That Constitute Forgiveness

Applying these conditions to the presuppositions of forgiveness discussed in the preceding section yields the following analysis. We have already seen that, in expressing forgiveness of an agent X for his act A, a speaker S represents as true the following statements: (1) X did A; (2) A was wrong; (3) X was responsible for doing A; (4) S was personally injured by X's doing A; and (5) S resented being injured by X's doing A. These statements S must represent in expressing forgiveness, and they must be true to prevent a misfire. They are, to again quote William Alston, the judgments S must "take responsibility for holding" to express a state of mind linguistically.[93] But we have said that this also must be represented: (6) S has overcome his resentment for X's doing A, or is at least willing to try to overcome it. Must this likewise be true to prevent a misfire? Or does its falsity result only in an abuse or breach of commitment? The answer is far from obvious.

One reason for thinking that the falsity of (6) does *not* prevent "I forgive you" from taking effect is that "I forgive you" is a procedure "designed for use by persons having certain thoughts or feelings." This being so, it should follow that, when S says "I forgive you" without representing that he has overcome his resentment, he would nonetheless succeed in expressing his attitude. To be sure, he would *abuse* the formula—for which abuse he could be censured—but it would not follow that he failed to express forgiveness. The most we could say is that S had no business uttering the formula in the first place.

It is indeed tempting to say that the falsity of (6) does not prevent the formula's taking place—if only because, as we have seen, it is possible to forgive in the presence of resentment. However, intuitively we find this explanation too pallid to cover the whole story of what it means to express forgiveness. Out of our own experience in forgiving and being forgiven, we are bound to object, "What about the way it *feels* to forgive someone?!" The force of this objection is that (6) should be counted among those conditions that are *constitutive* of forgiveness, by which is meant that, should (6) be false, S does not succeed in forgiving at all.

However, having the requisite feelings is only half the story of (6). If, as the statement allows, S has some residual resentment, then he still succeeds in avoiding a misfire so long as he will try to overcome it in the future. Thus, if S *sincerely intends* to will away his resentment, then he *does* succeed in expressing forgiveness. If he should give up his effort at a later time, then—and only then—can we say his forgiveness was infelicitous, inasmuch as he has at that time breached his commitment to overcome resentment. According to this analysis, S succeeds in expressing forgiveness provided he has overcome his resentment; or, should resentment be present when the locution is uttered, S still succeeds provided he is willing to overcome it in the future. The locution misfires only when S has not overcome resentment and is not willing to try to do so in the future. In this sense we *can* count (6) among the representations S must make in expressing forgiveness.

An additional argument for placing (6) among the statements S must represent in expressing forgiveness concerns the effect S's saying "I forgive you" has on the wrongdoer. In his later writings, Austin abandoned his distinction between performatives and statements (or "constatives," as he called them) and replaced it with his theory of illocutionary forces. Under the terms of this theory, whenever someone says something, he performs a number of distinguishable acts. In addition to the *phonetic* act of making certain sounds and the *phatic* act of uttering words in accordance with grammar, Austin distinguished three other kinds of acts that we may perform when we say something. First, we may perform the *locutionary* act of using an utterance with a certain sense of reference. Second, we may perform the *illocutionary* act, which is the act we are performing in performing the locutionary act. Third, we may perform the *perlocutionary* act, which is the communicative act we may succeed in performing by means of the illocutionary act. Thus, when a speaker says, "The door is open," he is performing the locutionary act of referring to a specified door. But he may also be performing the illocutionary act of hinting that the door is open. And by performing the illocutionary act of hinting that the door is open, he may succeed in performing the perlocutionary act of getting the listener to close it.[94]

Employing this analysis, we may now say that when S says "I forgive you," in addition to performing the illocutionary act of expressing forgiveness, he is also performing the perlocutionary act of inviting the listener to believe that he is forgiven. Certainly, this is what the listener must think if S utters the formula sincerely. We have seen, though, that this may not be what S intends in saying to X, "I forgive you." As R. J. O'Shaughnessy pointed out, S may be performing such perlocutionary acts as retaliating against X for an earlier incident.[95] But under normal circumstances at least, it is quite reasonable for X to believe that the perlocutionary force of S's utterance is to get X to believe that he is indeed forgiven. X would naturally count this as the *behabitive force*.[96] Thus, the perlocutionary effect of being forgiven must ordinarily be thought to be correlated with the illocutionary act of expressing forgiveness.

Admittedly, placing (6) among the conditions that are constitutive of expressing forgiveness does not fit neatly into Austin's scheme. Given the import of his fifth condition, it would seem that the falsity of (6) results in an abuse rather than a misfire. What does fit neatly is the resulting breach of commitment following S's abandoning the effort to overcome his resentment. This follows from Austin's sixth condition. Perhaps, in the final analysis, it is problems such as these that prompted Austin to have special misgivings about behabitives generally and is what led him to delcare that "in the field of behabitives, besides the usual liability to infelicities, there is a special scope for insincerity."[97]

So we see, then, that the full set of conditions that must be present for S to express forgiveness is the locution itself plus the six statements that S represents as true. Despite the problems encountered with (6), it is safe to say that, should *any* of statements (1) through (6) for some reason be false, the locution misfires, and S fails to express his attitude felicitously.

Virtues of the Model

Having thus put forward my own analysis, the question we must ask is, how—if at all—is it superior to alternative and competing ones? First of all, instead of viewing the relation between forgiveness and the world as something in vacuo—an approach that I attribute to others—we can now see forgiveness as involving an intentional action by a speaker employing a conventional device (the words "I forgive you") in accordance with rules for the employment of this device.[98] These latter, of course, are the six statements that S represents as true. This being so, then—qua act—forgiveness is no longer susceptible to the kinds of criticisms to which *definitions* of forgiveness are susceptible. Thus, rather than struggling with the meaning of forgiveness (which meaning is thought to be captured by necessary and sufficient conditions), this analysis recasts the discussion into the larger context of forgiving behavior. The question "What is forgiveness?" can be seen and answered in the context of what speakers mean when they employ the term. Once one sees forgiveness as an action that is performed in the utterance of an expression with a particular sense provided by the rules for using the expression, then it is easier to see that it is subject to the sorts of errors that plague—not concepts—but actions in general.[99]

What are such errors? From what has been said thus far, one would think that the only thing "I forgive you" must do is to be felicitous, take effect, not misfire, and not be abused. But that is not all. There are other questions, equally important, that we want to ask about this act. We want to know, for instance, whether forgiveness is an act that one is obligated to perform. If the answer is yes, then we will want also to know whether the obligation is strict or loose. In addition, we want to know whether there are times one deserves to be forgiven, or whether forgiveness is always at the discretion of the victim; whether there are any acts that are in principle unforgiveable; and so on and so forth. Approaching forgiveness as an act allows us to ask precisely these questions to which we intuitively want answers.

There are other virtues of my analysis as well. Recall that a major objection to the model of forgiveness as the overcoming of resentment is the need to distinguish between putative forgiveness and true forgiveness. A moment's reflection will show that, in my analysis, this problem does not arise. If a necessary condition of forgiveness is the overcoming of resentment, then if S forgives X it is *true* that S bears him no grudge, and false otherwise. This is the result of focusing on the word "forgiveness" as incarnated in the sentence "S forgives X." In my analysis, one way for S to forgive X is to *say* felicitously that he forgives him—at which time S represents that he has overcome his resentment or, if not, that he is willing to try to overcome it. As long as what S represents is true, then, should it turn out that S still resents X, the act of forgiveness has nonetheless taken place. Thus, one of the virtues of my analysis is that it makes forgiveness far easier than we might otherwise have thought. Indeed, one might say my analysis acknowledges that not only is it human to err, but it is human to forgive as well. To acknowledge this is to say that forgiveness has a place in our moral lives, which is what we suspected all along.

Another criticism we made of the model that construes forgiveness as the overcoming of resentment is the asymmetry it imposes between forgiving and being forgiven. In this view, a wrongdoer's reception of forgiveness can always be defeated by his victim's subsequent resentment, despite the wrongdoer's reasonable belief to the contrary at the time of being forgiven. In my analysis, a wrongdoer is forgiven when he is felicitously told that he is forgiven. Subsequent resentment following the expression of forgiveness does not, in my view, undermine forgiveness, so long as there exists the forgiver's commitment to try to eliminate what resentment remains.

Finally, in my account of forgiveness, there is no danger of confusing it with natural or therapeutic forgetting, which criticism we targeted at Horsbrugh. Expressing forgiveness cannot be confused with forgetting, if only because forgiveness is intentional in a way that forgetting is not. Thus, forgiveness as a speech act lends meaning to "forgive and forget" in a way that alternative views do not. In sum, what I have been arguing for is a conception of forgiveness that satisfies our intuitions about what it is, without the difficulties that others engender.[100]

In saying all this, I do not mean to imply that my analysis of forgiveness does not yield surprising results. That it does so is evidenced by the fact that "I forgive you" is a speech act. Since this is so, it turns out that forgiveness is more like promising than we would otherwise suspect: If we sincerely say "I promise to," we represent, inter alia, that we intend to keep our promise. However, subsequent failure to keep our promise does not prevent the promise from taking effect. Likewise, if we sincerely say "I forgive you," we represent that, where resentment is still present, we intend to overcome it at some later point in time; but failure to overcome it does not prevent our forgiveness from having taken effect. Certainly, there are important dissimilarities between forgiving and promising, but my analysis of forgiveness does reveal some interesting analogies that might otherwise be concealed.

To be sure, many philosophers who have considered forgiveness deny that "I forgive you" is like "I promise to" in relevant respects. According to Kathleen Dean Moore, "saying 'I forgive you' may be like saying 'I promise you,' in that the listener expects certain characteristic ways of acting to follow the locution; however, unless a change of attitude follows or accompanies the words, no forgiving can be said to have taken place."[101] Here, Moore is following Murphy and others who define forgiveness as the overcoming of resentment. As I see it, if a speaker has felicitously expressed forgiveness, then should he not have overcome his resentment—that is, changed his attitude—he has nonetheless forgiven, provided he is willing to try to do so in the future.

In Horsbrugh's account, "I forgive you" is not a performative—mainly, he explains, because we sometimes say "I'll try to forgive you," and one cannot use the verb "to try" in connection with a performative.[102] Ostensibly, what Horsbrugh means here is that we cannot use "to try" in connection with a performative because the simple uttering of the words in question is always within the immediate power of the agent. I would agree that this much is true. However, a *sincere* utterance of the words in question is not always within the power of the agent. This being so, it makes perfect sense to use "to try" with such performatives as "I welcome," "I congratulate," "I do" (take this woman, etc.), and so forth. All of these locutions are examples of what Austin himself took to be performatives.[103] Thus, it makes perfect sense to *try* to say "I welcome you" to one whom we do not like very much, to *try* to say "I congratulate you" to one whose good fortune we do not think is deserved, and to *try* to say "I do" to one whom we have reservations about marrying. Because of this, I see no reason why we cannot *try* to say "I forgive you" in those cases where the very saying of it is difficult to do.[104]

Finally, R. S. Downie has this to say about the analogy of forgiveness with promising:

> The uttering of these words ["I forgive you"] or their equivalent, is certainly not sufficient to constitute forgiveness. Unless the words are accompanied by the appropriate behavior we shall say that A has not really forgiven B. In this respect, forgiving differs from promising. Whereas the utterance of "I promise" does, at least in most circumstances, constitute a promise though the appropriate behavior is not forthcoming, the utterance of "I forgive you" does not constitute forgiveness unless the appropriate behavior is forthcoming. It is true that forgiving is like promising in that to say "I forgive you" is to raise certain expectations which may or may not be fulfilled. But if the expectations are not fulfilled in the case of promising it is still true that a promise has been given, although a false one, whereas if they are not fulfilled in the case of forgiving we do not allow that there has been forgiveness at all.[105]

This analysis, besides being blind to "I forgive you" as a behabitive, is similar to Moore's and open to similar objections.

To conclude, I have endeavored to show that it is easy to believe that the meaning of forgiveness can be captured in a straitjacket of necessary and sufficient conditions, if we presume that saying "I forgive you" never alone constitutes forgiveness. However, this approach leads us to models of forgiveness with serious flaws. Thus, rather than ruling out a priori that "I forgive you" can be a performative, I have sought to show that such a construction is not only possible—belonging to the class of behabitives—but that it is also powerful as an explanatory tool.

Of course, nothing I have said thus far shows that forgiveness is a virtue. Having analyzed the concept, I have left open the question as to whether and to what extent one *ought* to forgive. Perhaps, as we shall see, there are good reasons to forgive and good reasons not to. Before I consider this and related questions, it will be helpful to distinguish forgiveness from other concepts with which it is related but often confused. I turn, then, to consider what distinctions exist between forgiveness on the one hand, and condonation, pardon, and mercy on the other.

3

Other Things Forgiveness Is Not

Our concern in Chapter 1 was in analyzing models of forgiveness that, for one reason or another, do not stand up to scrutiny. Having proposed in Chapter 2 a model of forgiveness that ostensibly does stand up to scrutiny, our concern will now be to distinguish it from other concepts with which it is sometimes confused. These are, respectively, condonation, pardon, and mercy.

Condonation

It is easy to see how forgiveness is sometimes confused with condonation.[1] Webster's defines "condonation" to mean "the act of condoning, esp. of implying forgiveness"; and the term derives from the Latin *donare*, which means "to present or give." However, there are important—if subtle—differences between condonation and forgiveness. As in forgiveness, when someone condones another person's behavior, he represents that it is wrong and that the person is morally responsible. Aurel Kolnai and Jean Hampton also seem to think that the act of condonation presupposes personal injury to the one who is condoning,[2] but I think they are mistaken about this. I think that we can condone what is not a personal injury to ourselves but an injury to someone else—and not necessarily one with whom we identify. However, I think they are correct in maintaining that, unlike forgiveness, condonation does not presuppose resentment in any shape or form. Hampton defines condonation as "the acceptance, without moral protest (either inward or outward), of an action which ought to warrant such protest."[3] And Kolnai sees condonation as a sort of "emotional prescription."[4] As Kolnai understands it, when we condone someone's immoral behavior, we acquiesce to the offense, perhaps because of the wrongdoer's merits or virtues in other respects, perhaps because of tolerance of human nature, and so forth. Condonation is, he says, unlike exculpation and justification—which forgiveness is also unlike—but is more akin to excuse in the Austinian sense of absolving a person's wrongdoing in virtue of mitigating circumstances.[5]

We see, then, that the essential difference between forgiveness and condonation is that forgiveness presupposes personal injury, which one protests against in the form of resentment, while condonation does not presuppose personal injury (or at least not necessarily, contra Hampton and Kolnai) and in any event does not presuppose the protest of resentment. In fact, of necessity, condonation precludes such a protest. Furthermore, when we condone an action, we do so immediately—unlike when we forgive someone, which often takes place over a period of time. Thus, condonation is very much like forgiveness, but is sufficiently distinct as to require separate analysis.

Pardon

With respect to the concepts of pardon and mercy, it is easy to see how these concepts also are conflated with forgiveness. Sir Edward Coke's definition of "pardon," for example, is as follows: "A pardon is a work of *mercy* whereby the king . . . *forgiveth* any crime, offense, punishment, etc."[6] Herbert Morris refers to pardon as the "legal analogue" of forgiveness.[7] But again, the concept of forgiveness is best kept distinguished from both pardon and mercy.

Jeffrie Murphy explains, "To pardon someone is not simply to change the way one feels about him [contra forgiveness] but to let him avoid what may well be his just deserts."[8] Murphy mentions as an example Gerald Ford's pardon of Richard Nixon—an example Susan Jacoby uses not to exemplify pardoning per se but to evince what forgiveness is *not*.[9] To Kathleen Dean Moore, "a pardon is an act by the executive officer (or others legally empowered) that lessens or eliminates a punishment determined by a court of law, or which changes the punishment in a way usually regarded as mitigating."[10] According to R. S. Downie, "to pardon a person . . . is to let him off the merited consequences of his actions; it is to overlook what he has done and to treat him with indulgence."[11] Downie adds that a pardon necessarily issues from a figure in authority and necessarily for an offense against some normative order.[12]

As I see it, these conceptions of what a pardon is are correct in their essentials. This being so, we may say that the primary difference between pardoning and forgiving is that the former can issue only from one who is empowered to do so. In other words, only an authority formally so constituted within a legal system or other system of normative rules is qualified to pardon. Forgiving, however, is something we do as *individuals*. Thus, we pardon as officials in social roles, but forgive as persons qua persons.

There are further differences. In pardoning an individual, we represent that we will either forgo or mitigate punishment that is otherwise deserved. Unlike in forgiveness, we represent this necessarily.[13] Furthermore, we pardon individuals for offenses committed against a normative order other than the moral order.[14] An example of this is Ford's pardon of Nixon, but a club official can also pardon an erring club member for violating its rules.[15]

But if there are essential differences between pardoning and forgiving, there are also similarities. As I see it, "I pardon you" is, like "I forgive you," a performative utterance (see Chapter 2). Of course, the appropriate circumstances under which these formulas take effect are different. Had Spiro Agnew said to Nixon, "I pardon you," his performative would have misfired, as he was not in a position to perform this act. Furthermore, "I pardon you" belongs to the class of what J. L. Austin called "exercitives."[16] "An exercitive is the giving of a decision in favour of or against a certain course of action, or advocacy of it."[17] In addition to pardoning, Austin mentions "appointing," "voting," "ordering," "urging," "advising," and "warning" as examples of exercitives.[18] However, exercitives do share some features in common with behabitives. Certain exercitives ("challenging," "protesting," "approving," etc.) may consist in the taking up of an attitude or the performing of an act.[19] To this extent, "I pardon you" and "I forgive you" are rather alike.

The most interesting point in this account of mine (after Austin) is that "I forgive you" and "I pardon you" are both performatives—a view not shared by either Downie or Moore. As Downie sees it, "I pardon you" is indeed a performative when uttered by a person in authority since, by uttering the formula, he sets in motion the normative machinery whereby the offense will be overlooked. But in saying "I forgive you," the forgiver does not, in a similar way, set anything in motion; he is signaling that he has the appropriate attitude and that the wrongdoer can expect appropriate behavior.[20] Moore would agree with this claim.[21] But both writers subscribe to the view that forgiveness is essentially the overcoming of resentment—a view that I do not share.

Another and very interesting similarity emerges if we construe punishment, as Henry Sidgwick did, to be "resentment universalized"[22] and go on to say that a pardon entails the remission of punishment. If we construe punishment along these lines, we can then say that, in pardoning someone, an official represents that the public has overcome resentment or is willing to try to do so. In this sense, the official is expressing an attitude very much like an individual does when he expresses forgiveness.

But there is more to be said about what a pardon is. In one view, a pardon presupposes wrongdoing, as illustrated by this statement from the dicta of *Burdick v. United States*:

> This brings us to the difference between legislative immunity and pardon. They [sic] are substantial. The latter carries an imputation of guilt.[23]

In other views, a pardon does not presuppose wrongdoing at all. Moore's definitional analysis of the pardon is thoroughly positivistic. As she sees it, "pardons imply, not guilt, but legal or moral innocence or both."[24]

It is beyond the scope of this chapter to follow the twists and turns of the arguments for and against these views. The main point is that, however we construe the concept of pardon, it is sufficiently dissimilar to the concept of forgiveness as to make it a conceptual error to conflate the two.

Mercy

Finally, with respect to "What is mercy?" two distinct questions pervade the literature. First, there is the question of what mercy is, construed as a quality of *judges*. Second, there is the question of what mercy is, construed as a quality of *individuals*. However, whether we approach mercy as a quality of judges or of individuals, it will be seen that mercy and forgiveness are conceptually distinguishable.

In her celebrated article "Mercy," Alwynne Smart is concerned to give an adequate account of mercy as a quality that is shown by judges.[25] She asks the following complex of questions: "What are the conditions for the appropriate exercising of mercy, how do we decide how much mercy is appropriate, and when is a judge morally obliged to be merciful, if ever?''[26] In the first part of the article, Smart puts on one side such things as a jury's recommendation of mercy and pleas for mercy on the grounds of mitigating circumstances. She maintains that such cases of ''mercy'' are misnamed, for to her this is nothing more than a way of ensuring *justice*. Smart says, ''When a man exercises mercy what he does is acknowledge that an offense has been committed, decides that a particular punishment would be appropriate or just, and then decides to exact a punishment of lesser severity than the appropriate or just one.''[27]

Thus, the thesis Smart wishes to defend is that, with certain exceptions, showing mercy is either *unjust* or it is not mercy we are talking about. Mercy—if it is truly mercy we are referring to—is justified only in the extreme case when a judge is compelled to mitigate a punishment by the overriding claims of other moral obligations—such as, for example, the obligation to prevent inflicting undeserved suffering on the offender's family. When judges display mercy, they appeal to what they view as proper and just punishment. However, in so doing, they fail to do what the law requires—namely, to treat like cases in a like manner. What follows from this is that they commit an injustice to other wrongdoers. Therefore, in the few cases where mercy can be justified, it can be justified only by appealing to a multidimensional moral theory that provides for the claims other moral obligations have on us.[28]

In a critique of Smart, Claudia Card has argued that we do not need to introduce conflicting moral obligations to make sense of mercy.[29] As she sees it, the obligations of justice are sufficient to justify a judge's showing of mercy. Card argues that punishment and mercy are both just responses to the wrongdoer's desert. In contrast to Smart, Card argues that tempering justice with mercy ensures us that the legally permissible punishment does not exceed the amount of suffering the wrongdoer deserves, all things considered.[30]

For present purposes, the theses of both Smart and Card are of less interest than is their assumption that mercy is a quality of judges shown in a court of law—specifically, the criminal court of law. If what they mean by this is that mercy is a quality *peculiar* to judges, then—whatever else one may say about this view—mercy is not easily mistaken for forgiveness, if only because we forgive as individuals. Furthermore, in both their theses, showing mercy essentially involves mitigating a punishment that the wrongdoer deserves. As we have already seen above and in Chapter 1, forgiveness need not entail the mitigation of a punishment. Finally, while in Smart's account, at least, mercy often turns out to be a vice rather than a virtue, forgiveness is ordinarily thought of as a virtuous quality.

P. Twambley, whose article "Mercy and Forgiveness" is in part a critique of Smart's position, understands Smart to be indeed arguing that mercy is a quality unique to judges.[31] However, as Twambley sees it,

> Mrs. Smart was not altogether mistaken in going to court to understand mercy, but I suggest that she has gone to the wrong court. Not the criminal court, but the *civil* court, is where we will find an adequate model for mercy.[32]

In going to the civil court to find his adequate model, Twambley argues that "the exercise of mercy consists in the plaintiff waiving his right over the defendant and thus releasing him from his 'bond.' "[33] Citing favorably from *The Merchant of Venice* (which, notes Twambley, contains the most celebrated eulogy of mercy in the English language), Twambley points out that it is Shylock, the plaintiff—and not the judge—whom Portia bids temper justice with mercy.[34] Employing this model, Twambley contends that "one man shows mercy to another when he waives his right over that person and releases him from his obligation."[35] This model is also shared by Jeffrie Murphy, who is concerned with constructing a model of mercy that allows us to give it meaning as an autonomous virtue.[36] Like Twambley, Murphy sees what he calls the "Private Law Paradigm" as avoiding the problems engendered by Smart's account.

If we accept the Private Law Paradigm as a correct model of mercy, then what follows from this is that the essence of mercy lies in the waiving of a right we could in justice assert. This being so, showing mercy is not something one need do in an institutional role. Murphy observes, "A litigant in a civil suit is not the occupier—in anything like the same sense—of an institutional role. He occupies a private role."[37] Notwithstanding the fact that the plaintiff in a legal action may indeed be said to occupy an institutional role, a run-of-the-mill creditor may certainly show mercy by releasing his run-of-the-mill debtor from the debt owed or—what is the same thing—waive the right he could in justice assert. Thus, as a model of mercy, the Private Law Paradigm has advantages over the "Criminal Law Paradigm," as it allows us to take mercy out of the courtroom.

From my point of view, Twambley and Murphy are correct in arguing that the essence of mercy lies in the waiving of a right that we could in justice assert.[38] However, I would add to this that the waiving of such a right must be done for reasons having to do with pity or compassion.[39] This being so, then, contra Smart and Card, mercy need not be construed as the exclusive property of judges—that is, those who have the authority to punish—if indeed this is what they are claiming. What remains to be seen, is how forgiveness differs from mercy where the latter is construed as a quality of individuals.

As I see it, the main difference between mercy and forgiveness is in that to which we are waiving a right. In mercy, we waive the right to whatever it is we have a right to. In forgiveness—more specifically—we waive the "right" to resent the wrongdoer. Furthermore, unlike mercy—where, when we waive the right to the thing owed, the matter is a fait accompli—when we waive the right to resentment in forgiveness, we may continue to harbor negative feelings. Thus, while we cannot show mercy and at the same time insist on collecting our debt, we can forgive and also resent so long as we are willing to overcome our resentment.

To be sure, if there are differences between mercy and forgiveness, there are also similarities. In showing mercy and forgiving, we ordinarily represent that the wrongdoer committed a wrong for which he is responsible and for which he deserves appropriate treatment, be it punishment in the case of mercy or resentment in the case of forgiveness. We also represent that, because of other considerations, we will not impose the treatment that is deserved. However, it should be clear by now that, despite their similarities, forgiveness is distinct from mercy and has a logic of its own.

Part II

When We Should and Should Not Forgive

4

The Ethics of Resentment

Consider the story (from a popular book on forgiveness) of a couple who visited a prison to embrace in forgiveness "Tom," the man who had raped and murdered their twenty-two-year-old daughter. In this book, the parents tell of the horror and pain they felt in learning of their daughter's death. Eventually, however, fortified with a deep sense of religiosity, they decide to leave retribution to heaven and forgive their enemy for his sins.

The mother of the victim describes their meeting in prison as follows:

> The door opened; Tom entered the room. He was about 6 feet tall, dark-haired and muscular, cleanly dressed and shaven . . . a person. God's love welled up within me and overflowed. Tom paused, his eyes filled up with tears. My husband and I stood and each in turn embraced Tom. We wept together.[1]

I have no comments to make on the religious significance of this event. I put this story at the head of my discussion of the ethics of resentment because it illustrates a disquieting feature of forgiving behavior. From one perspective, the parents' forgiveness of their daughter's wrongdoer connotes great love, warmth, and compassion. It suggests a letting go, a release—an action that has the power to soothe, heal, and restore. But from another perspective, the parents' forgiveness portrays them to be unfeeling, unloving, and disrespectful of their daughter's worth. Not knowing the conditions under which the forgiveness was tendered (e.g., did the wrongdoer repent? did he offer to make amends?), we cannot help but regard their forgiveness as not so morally good and unambiguously a virtue as it might otherwise appear to be.

In a recent paper on forgiveness, Jeffrie Murphy defended the

Nietzschean position that forgiveness may, at least in certain circumstances, be harmful and wrong—a vice rather than a virtue.[2] Following Bishop Joseph Butler, Murphy understands forgiveness to be the overcoming of resentment.[3] And resentment, according to Murphy, is not necessarily a bad thing. It is, as he says at one point, "the natural, fitting, and proper response to certain instances of wrongdoing."[4] What follows, if he is correct, is that we should sometimes harbor resentment rather than overcome it. Which is to say that sometimes we ought not to forgive.

Working backward from resentment to forgiveness, I shall argue, following Murphy, that resentment is the proper response to personal injury and that the failure to resent under certain circumstances is indicative of a moral defect. This being so, I shall go on to argue that we ought not to forgive a responsible wrongdoer unless for a reason that is morally appropriate. My thesis in this section is that forgiveness is appropriate insofar as it is permissible from the moral point of view and not ruled out by moral considerations.

In Defense of Resentment

In suggesting that resentment may be the proper response to personal injury, I am going against the popular view that resentment is a negative feeling. Robert Solomon, for one, echoes the popular view when he refers to resentment as "among the most obsessive and enduring of the emotions, poisoning the whole of subjectivity with its venom, often achieving moodlike scope while still maintaining its keen and vicious focus on each of the myriad of petty offenses it senses against itself."[5] However, despite the eloquence of Solomon's indictment, there are reasons to believe it is anything but true.

Butler, as we have seen, raised the question of how a benevolent deity could implant in us so unloving a passion as resentment. On the face of it, resentment is a passion that is unambiguously evil. However, according to Butler, the reason that resentment arouses our suspicion is that it is often directed at trivial affronts rather than real moral injury, and sometimes it provokes excessive behavior. But as Butler pointed out, it would be a mistake to condemn resentment because it admits of irrational extensions. So too does love, for that matter. Thus, it is not resentment per se that is evil, but its tendency to get out of hand and cause us to act in immoral ways.

Murphy agrees with Butler that resentment may have undesirable consequences in action. "Resentment," Murphy says, " . . . may have something to do with our willingness to let prisons remain the inhuman pestholes they now tend to be. . . . [I]t is also an obstacle to the restoration of equal moral relations among persons."[6] Thus, as a consequence of harboring resentment, it is impossible to ever have "the kind of intimate relationships that are one of the crowning delights of human existence."[7] However, Murphy is quick to point out that this is true of *excessive* resentment, or anger that is *not* justified.[8]

In distinguishing between anger that is justified and anger that is not, we have an additional clue as to why resentment is not so unsavory as might otherwise be thought. Resentment, as I have explained in Chapter 2, is anger that one may *properly* feel on being personally injured. It is anger, says Murphy, "that might be felt, for example, by former inmates of a concentration camp toward a former camp commandant . . . or by those American soldiers—now dying of cancer—toward those who negligently exposed them to radiation during atomic testing."[9] Thus, if a case is to be made against resentment, it must be made against *justified* anger and not against unjustified anger or anger that is excessive.

Examples of the latter abound in literature. In Graham Greene's *The Tenth Man*, for instance, the sister of Janvier Mangeot spends several years doing little more than anticipating the arrival of Jean-Louis Chavel who, while imprisoned during the Nazi occupation of Paris, had sold his estate to Mangeot in exchange for Mangeot's being one of ten men to be executed. Thinking that Chavel will one day return, Theresa Mangeot waits by the window day after day, consumed by her excessive desire to spit in his face and perhaps even kill the hated Chavel.[10] We also have the biblical account of Saul's jealous anger toward David—which was not justified, as David had inflicted no moral injury on Saul.[11] To this, I might add Javert's anger toward Jean Valjean in *Les Miserables*—an anger that was all too consuming and hardly justified.[12]

These examples aside, resentment is—as Norvin Richards rightly puts it—"a disposition which varies considerably in its intensity and in the length of its natural tenure."[13] Because of this, we can safely say that Robert Solomon's indictment is not anything like an indictment of resentment in its normal form. "Think here," says Richards, "of the parent who is angry at the child for disobeying, but is certainly not transformed into a spiteful, single-minded avenger."[14] In a word, what Murphy said about *hatred* applies, mutatis mutandis, to resentment:

> It is striking the degree to which those who wish to give hatred a bad name tend to focus on examples either of hatred that is not retributive or of retributive hatred that is clearly unjustified because the person hated is in fact (the hater's beliefs to the contrary) not really guilty of any unjust conduct.[15]

It may also be said that Solomon is describing not resentment but *vindictiveness*—an emotion phenomenologically different. Unlike resentment, vindictiveness has—as constitutive of its very nature—the desire to get even, which cannot be said of resentment in its normal form. Karen Horney, for one, echoes this thought when she says that "the vindictive person . . . is egocentric . . . because he has more or less severed his emotional relations to other human beings."[16] However, as I have previously argued, to resent someone is to feel anger that is deserved; and how much is deserved depends, among other things, on the nature of the wrong that has been committed.

Having said this, we may now ascertain what it is about resentment that makes it desirable as a moral response. Murphy says, "If I count morally as much as anyone else (as surely I do), a failure to resent moral injuries done to me is a failure to care about the moral value incarnate in my own moral personality (that I am, in Kantian language, an end-in-myself) and a failure to care about the very rules of morality."[17] Thus, he adds, "Just as the pyschopath who feels no guilt, shame, or remorse for the wrong he does can be said to lack a true appreciation of morality, so too can the person who feels no . . . resentment be said to lack a true appreciation of morality."[18] Andrew von Hirsch and Nils Jareborg put it this way:

> In situations of resentment . . . the role of the moral sense . . . becomes the spur as well as the bridle to the passions. Having been wronged, one is *properly* angry. Far from having a purely suppressing role, one's sense of right and wrong is part of what prompts and gives legitimacy to the anger.[19]

So, too, John Rawls refers to resentment as a "moral feeling [that] invokes[s] the concept of right."[20] Michael Moore argues that, "by repressing anger at wrongful violation, we may be attempting to deny that we live in a society in which there really are fearful and awful people."[21]

What follows from this is that a person who is self-respecting and who cares about the moral law will care about people (herself included) who are the objects of moral judgment, and she will express this care in the form of resentment when she is the object of moral injury. Not to do so is to leave herself open to those objections that Thomas Hill has leveled at the servile person, to wit: "The servile person displays this absence of self-respect . . . by acting as if his rights were nonexistent or insignificant."[22] Aristotle had this to say of the failure to feel anger when anger is warranted:

> The deficiency—a sort of inirascibility or whatever it is—is blamed, since people who are not angered by the right things, or in the right way, or at the right times, or towards the right people, all seem to be foolish. For such a person seems to be insensible and to feel no pain. Since he is not angered, he does not seem to be the sort to defend himself; and such willingness to accept insults to oneself or to overlook insults to one's family and friends is slavish.[23]

Thus, far from being concerned only about how we should act, morality—as Bernard Williams puts it—is

> about what a man ought or ought not to feel in certain circumstances, or, more broadly, about the ways in which various emotions may be considered as distinctive, mean or hateful, while others appear as creative, generous, admirable, or—merely—such as one would hope for from a decent human being.[24]

In saying this, Williams is echoing the ancient view, held by Aristotle, that the moral life of a creature having both rational and affective qualities involves the right ordering of both these elements. Aristotle stated his view in this way:

> I mean moral virtue; for it is this that is concerned with passions and actions, and in these there is excess, defect, and the intermediate. For instance, both fear and confidence and appetite and anger and pity and in general pleasure and pain may be felt both too much and too little, and in both cases not well; but to feel them at the right times, with reference to the right objects, toward the right people, with the right motive, and in the right way, is what is both intermediate and best, and this is characteristic of virtue.[25]

To be sure, there are those who would deny that morality is about what one should feel. What one ought to do is ordinarily thought to concern actions, which can be performed at will, while feelings are usually regarded as passions—states not subject to the will. In his *Metaphysical Principles of Virtue*, for example, Kant argues that we have no obligations to feel love and pity; the reason he gives is that feelings, unlike actions, cannot be commanded and made subject to the will. Obligations not to hate or envy others seem also to be denied on similar grounds, though Kant admits that we have obligations not to interfere with the happiness of others. This leads him to interpret moral principles that appear to concern feelings as actually concerning actions. Thus, Kant writes,

> Love is a matter of sensation, not of willing; and I cannot love because I would, still less because I should (being obligated to love). Hence a duty to love is nonexistent. But benevolence (*amor benevolentiae*), as a mode of action, can be subject to a law of duty. Disinterested benevolence toward men is often (though very improperly) called love.[26]

While Kant admits that "moderation in emotions and passions, self-control, and calm deliberation not only are good in many respects, but even seem to constitute a part of the inner worth of the person,"[27] even here he is talking about the *cultivation* and *control* of emotions, which can be voluntarily undertaken. He is not, however, talking of the duty to have the emotions or not.[28] Thus—according to Kant at least—if we have an obligation at all regarding the emotions, we are merely obligated to learn to control them. A corollary of this is that the emotions as such do not contribute to the moral worth of persons. It remains to be seen then—Williams aside—how and in what sense we ought to feel resentment against one who has injured us.

Feeling Resentment

As was mentioned earlier, the recent history of moral philosophy has placed great emphasis on action-based theories of right and wrong conduct. On the one hand, there are deontologists such as Kant who determine what we ought to do by seeing whether our actions are universalizable.[29] On the other hand, there are utilitarians such as Mill who determine what we ought to do by seeing whether our actions maximize happiness.[30] G. E. Moore, also a utilitiarian, defined right action in terms of the good, but unlike Mill denied that the only kind of consequence to be taken into account is the pleasure that our acts produce.[31] But whatever the differences among these theorists, all discuss moral goods and evils by focusing on actions or principles that are good or evil. They do not emphasize the person who performs the actions, has motives, and follows principles through the temporal narration of her life. Because of this, action-based theories leave little room for the affective life in the moral world. Where such theories do leave room for the affections at all, they are seen as entirely ancillary or incidental, helping us or hindering us from performing our duties.

Of late, however, attention has turned to the role of the affections, as philosphers have emphasized the significance of virtue. G. E. M. Anscombe[32] and George Henrik von Wright,[33] for example, called to our attention decades ago that virtue has become a neglected topic in modern ethics and challenged us to rediscover the contribution it can make to moral philosophy. More recently, philosophical probings have come from such people as Lawrence Becker,[34] Edmund Pincoffs,[35] James Wallace,[36] and, most notably, Alasdair MacIntyre.[37] Citing the judgments we commonly make about good and evil persons, their traits of character, and their willingness to perform certain kinds of actions, these philosophers call attention to the fact that we judge the moral worth of persons over time and not merely on whether they perform the right kinds of actions.

While it is beyond the scope of this book to assess the relative merits of an ethics of action as opposed to an ethics of virtue, it is worthwhile noting that some see the call to virtue as a summons to displace the focus on action in favor of a focus on character. Represented here are such people as Anscombe and MacIntyre. The latter, for instance, seem to suggest that rights, principles, duties, and the like should be *replaced* by the virtues as constituting in toto the only significant moral category. Others, like William Frankena[38] and Bernard Mayo,[39] see the call to virtue as a plea for balance and comprehensiveness in moral deliberations. Mayo, for instance, characterizes action-based theories as being too one-sided and shows how an ethics of virtue adds an important dimension to moral philosophy.

As I see it, virtue does have a place in moral philosophy, but not in lieu of action-guiding principles. In my estimation, we need a theory that, in addition to allowing us to evaluate agents, allows us to evaluate acts as well. Were we to limit ourselves to evaluating agents, our theory would fail for several reasons. For one, it would fail to provide guidance on the many issues of applied ethics, such as whether justice demands the imposition of the death penalty. For another, it would fail to allow us to list specific acts that for social reasons must be absolutely prohibited.[40] For reasons such as these, I believe that an ethics of virtue cannot stand alone and requires an ethics of action for balance and completeness.

In saying that we cannot get along with an ethics of virtue apart from an ethics of action, I have in no way indicated whether an ethics of virtue depends on an ethics of action, or the other way around. Some have given priority to virtue, while others argue the reverse. While both of these viewpoints have much to commend them, there is much to be said against them as well.[41] For my part, I agree with Frankena that, while an ethics of action is logically prior to an ethics of virtue, we need not construe them as rival moralities.[42] Tom Beauchamp has put it thusly: "A morality of principles . . . should enthusiastically recommend settled dispositions to act in accordance with that which is morally required, and a proponent of virtue ethics should encourage the development of principles that express how one ought to act."[43]

But why believe that an ethics of action is logically prior to an ethics of virtue? And why believe that an ethics of virtue adds something important to an ethics of action? As I see it, even if we could agree on those principles that are morally binding, an ethics of principle cannot get started without the disposition to act in accordance with them. This is the problem of "motivational skepticism," according to which, even if we could present a convincing account of how a particular moral principle is linked to the way terms like "right" are ordinarily used and how we may judge what things are right, it remains sensible to ask, "But why should I act that way?"[44] For the virtue theorist, this is hardly a problem. As Aristotle argued, principles are arrived at by reflection on activities that have been experienced prereflectively and internalized as dispositions.[45] If this is true, then we must, in addition to *knowing* what is right, *be moved to do* what is right. As Frankena so eloquently puts it, "principles without traits are impotent."[46]

Even so—if principles without traits are indeed impotent—"traits without principles are blind."[47] How, it could be asked, are we to determine which dispositions we ought to develop without prior knowledge of right and wrong conduct? Frankena says, "It is hard to see how we could know what traits to encourage or inculcate if we did not subscribe to principles, for example, to the principle of utility, or to those of benevolence and justice."[48] Thus, in my view, while an ethics of principle is logically prior to an ethics of virtue, we need an ethics of virtue for motivational purposes. Consequently, we have an adequate moral theory only when we join moral virtues to moral principles of right and wrong conduct.

I might further add that what are thought to be virtues are virtues of form only; they do not become *moral* virtues unless guided by moral principles. Take, for example, courage and sympathy. An individual can display great courage in serving an evil cause and can show unusual sympathy toward those who support the same cause. Hitler and Stalin are two of the many tyrants who have displayed these traits to a high degree. However, from my point of view, it is a mistake to associate the display of these traits with the display of *virtue* in such cases. As Philippa Foot has argued, from the fact that "X is a virtue" and "X is operating here," it does not follow that "X is operating here *as a virtue*."[49]

We see, then, that an ethics of action and an ethics of virtue are both vital to our understanding of morality. I propose, then—following Frankena—that we "regard the morality of principles and the morality of traits of character . . . as complementary. . . . Then, for every principle there will be a morally good trait, often going by the same name, consisting of a disposition or tendency to act according to it; and for every morally good trait there will be a principle defining the kind of action in which it is to express itself."[50]

Of course, the objection could be raised that there are points at which the correspondence between virtues and principles breaks down. Benevolence, for instance, is thought to be a virtue, although there is no principle that morally requires it.[51] How then could we argue that for every virtue there corresponds to it a principle of duty? To answer this question, it is important to be reminded that an ethics of principle encompasses not only actions that are required or enjoined, but also acts of supererogation. Thus, while it is true that we do not punish people for failing to be benevolent, and there are no acts that are uniquely associated with expressing benevolence, it does not follow that there is not a sense in which we *ought* to be benevolent. We ought to be benevolent notwithstanding that no one has a right to our benevolence. Once this is seen, it is clear how there can be a correspondence between virtues and principles.

However we construe the relationship between an ethics of action and an ethics of virtue, the point to be made is that there is a place for the virtues in moral theory. Take gratitude, for instance. Once again, it is true that we do not punish people for failing to be grateful; there is no specific act that must be done if we are to feel grateful, and there are no acts that one can demand in return for one's largess. But far from showing that gratitude has nothing to do with morality, such facts—if taken alone—bespeak an impoverished view of what it means to have a morality.[52] In addition to informing us how to behave in certain situations, morality is concerned with informing us how to feel at various times and what attitudes to take under relevant conditions. It counsels us, for instance, to be worried when a friend or relative is in a difficult situation, to be distressed over the ill fare of loved ones, to be joyous when great gains are made by those who are close to us. In a word, as Aristotle put it, morality is about passions as well as actions.

Having shown then that feelings and attitudes are relevant to morality, we can now see the context in which it makes sense to say that one ought to feel ———, where the blank is filled in by an emotional state. Consider the statement "You ought to feel sorry for the plight of the homeless," said to one indifferent to their cause. While not a demand that one should feel sorrow (no one has a *right* to another's sorrow), such a statement is a criticism of moral character. There is something lacking in an individual who is unmoved by the plight of the homeless. What this reveals is not a mere defect in personality. Feeling no sorrow for the plight of the homeless may rightly prompt moral castigation. Thus, while I am not morally *obligated* to feel sorrow in such cases, it does not follow that I am morally blameless if I am wholly indifferent to the misfortune.

Returning then to the feeling of resentment, it is now clear the sense in which the statement "You ought to feel resentment" has a place in our moral scheme. Not to feel resentment when resentment is called for is, as I have urged, a sign of servility, insofar as the victim conveys a lack of self-respect. This is because a principle of morality requires of people that they respect themselves. Otherwise put, to the principle of self-respect, there corresponds the virtue of resentment. Consequently, the failure to feel resentment when one has been injured is indicative of a moral defect.

There are, to be sure, views of resentment that are different still from this Kantian one. Mill, for instance, sees resentment as being linked not to self-respect, but to self-*defense*. In this respect, he has a rather biological interpretation of what it means to resent, as Mill himself acknowledges: "It is natural to resent . . . any harm done or attempted against ourselves . . . for every animal tries to hurt those who have hurt, or thinks are about to hurt, itself or its young."[53] Being an "impulse," as he calls it,[54] resentment is a response that is unreasoned and unreasoning.

From my perspective, Mill is confusing resentment, which is an idea-ridden response, with instinctive rage, which is a kind of primitive anger following an attack. Jean Hampton has written,

> A dog will snarl and bite back if it is bitten by a snake, and similarly a human being will feel a kind of attacking rage—a kind of "bite back" response—towards one who has "bitten" her when he has mistreated her. But dogs are not usually understood to be resentful (or at least not resentful in the way we are).[55]

Admittedly, resentment does have features in common with instinctive rage. Both, for instance, are responses to situations that are seen as in some way detrimental to well-being. However, unlike instinctive rage, which is best thought of as purely *conative*, resentment—in addition to having a conative structure—has a *cognitive* structure as well. Were this not the case (as Mill seems to think), we would be unable to evaluate people who feel and do not feel resentment. But since we do evaluate people in precisely this way, it follows that resentment is more than just a bite-back response.

True, one could still maintain that resentment lacks a cognitive content and explain its presence in us by making reference to its development in a social context. One could argue, for instance, that resentment exists in human beings so as to encourage cooperation among us by introducing a negative sanction for noncooperation. J. L. Mackie, for instance, explains "retribution" this way,[56] and Robert Axelrod says something like this in his discussion of what he calls "defection."[57] In this way, it could be said that resentment has been naturally selected for and refined in our highly social species. Neither are these two views—the cognitive and the social—incompatible with each other. That resentment serves as a defense of self-respect does not imply that it has not been selected out for survival as well.[58]

Expressing Resentment

If, as I have argued, there is a context in which it makes sense to say that one ought to feel resentment, it follows that certain actions have value as *expressions* of resentment. Certainly, we cannot drive an impenetrable wedge between how we feel and how we behave. Indeed, there is a sense in which one cannot be said to feel a certain way or have a certain attitude in the absence of characteristic behavior. Feelings and attitudes are expressed through behavior; and certain behaviors are the appropriate, concomitant expressions of certain feelings. Because of this, we may say that resentment has both internal and external aspects to it; the internal aspects have been dealt with above, and the external aspects shall be discussed below.

Before we address what it is that displays of resentment entail, however, it is important to mention that there are no particular acts that qualify as appropriate ones. Sometimes, resentment is expressed appropriately when we sever a relationship; other times it is expressed appropriately when we refuse to return a favor. There is no algorithm for deciding just what is appropriate and what is not, and it may be that there is no correct decision in the abstract—that it will depend on the nature of the relationship in question and on the degree of injury sustained. The point, however, is that, whatever does qualify as an appropriate expression of resentment, the action in question has value *as* an expression of resentment. As O. H. Green observes,

> the moral significance of actions must, often at least, be understood in terms of passions. Love and hatred are ethically important because they issue in acts of helping and hurting, but these are acts that are ethically important because they are acts of love and hatred, even apart from any benefit or harm done.[59]

Having said this, it is important to ascertain what it is exactly that gets expressed when we show resentment in any of its forms. It is tempting to say that, when we express resentment, we are simply giving vent to an internal state. After all, we speak of "feeling" resentful and having "feelings" of resentment. However, if this were all there was to the matter, it would not be very helpful in explaining why a failure to show resentment is, as I have urged, a moral deficiency. In addition, it would not help explain why the feeling of resentment should be proportionate to the way it is expressed, rather than to the intensity of one's feelings. Thus, it is important to give an account that will go some way toward dealing with these issues.

In Chapter 2, it will be recalled, I argued that resentment is essentially related to self-respect—that it is a response to personal moral injury perpetrated by a responsible moral agent. This being so, we should begin by noting that the commission of a moral injury against a particular victim evinces certain things about the agent who inflicts it—namely, that the agent is a wrongdoer, and the agent bears some degree of ill-will (or lack of good-will) toward the victim in question. Thus, in expressing her resentment of an agent X for X's act A, a victim V[60] represents the following statements:

(1) X did A;
(2) A was wrong;
(3) X was responsible for doing A; and
(4) V was personally injured by X's doing A.

Note that, with only a very minor change, these representations are essentially identical to those made by one who expresses *forgiveness*. Clearly, however, more is involved for both resentment and forgiveness alike. In addition to representing items (1) through (4), V, when expressing resentment, also represents the following:

(5) V has rights that V herself respects;
(6) X has rights that ought to be respected; and
(7) V has respect for the rules of morality, which mandate that we accord moral agents the respect they deserve.

Item (5) accounts for the idea that resentment is linked with self-respect. Items (6) and (7) require explanation at this juncture.

In Chapter 2, I argued that resentment—though essentially linked with self-respect—is also linked with respect for others as well as respect for the moral law. This, it will be recalled, is what distinguishes resentment from *indignation*—the latter being linked only with respect for others and respect for morality. This understood, when a victim V expresses her resentment of an agent X for X's act A, V not only shows that she respects herself, but she also shows that she respects X as well. Since resentment is always *of* an agent, an expression of resentment is a sign of respect for that agent in the rather peculiar way that Kant said we respect a murderer when we send the murderer to her rightful death. To show mercy to the murderer would be, according to Kant, to treat the murderer as a means to an end.[61] In a similar way, an expression of resentment shows X that V does not regard X solely as an instrument of V's own welfare, but as having value in X's own right. V shows this since it is required by the rules of morality.

To see this more clearly, recall our earlier discussion of the inappropriateness of resenting rocks when they fall on our feet (or cougars when they attack our children).[62] We said that resentment is inappropriate because rocks (and cougars) are not responsible moral agents. Wrongdoers, however, *are* moral agents and *are* capable of causing moral injury. Thus, to the extent that a display of resentment is a form of moral protest, we respect the wrongdoer when we voice our objection. The failure to do so is a sign that the wrongdoer is not taken seriously. In this sense, a victim V who expresses resentment represents not only that V deserves respect, but that the wrongdoer X deserves respect as well.

We see, then, that showing resentment conveys to a wrongdoer that we respect ourselves, others, and morality in general and that, for this reason, it is morally valuable as a response to injury. Furthermore, the display of resentment may also help foster a sense of *community* when it works to inspire moral reform. Seeing that her victim protests the injury, the wrongdoer may regret her behavior and vow to refrain from repeating it again.[63] Thus, in addition to being intrinsically valuable, a display of resentment also has value as an instrument of change. Of course, it hardly needs saying that only certain forms of showing resentment are morally valuable. There are some forms of showing resentment (e.g., taking revenge) that are morally prohibited.

If this account is correct, then expressions of resentment are demonstrations of a complex of beliefs, feelings, and attitudes. By showing resentment for the malevolence of others, we express the belief that they acted without our interests in mind and that we were injured by such actions; we express our feelings for the welfare of the wrongdoer—i.e., we take her seriously by not condoning what she did—and we indicate that we have an attitude of regard for wrongdoers, in the sense that we do not look on them as things whose movements happened to cause us injury. What follows from this is that the display of resentment has value insofar as it demonstrates an attitude appropriate to members of the moral community.

Justifying Resentment

We see, then, that—far from being a vice—resentment has many qualities to recommend it. Still, given its propensity to irrational extensions, we must, as Rawls has pointed out, be prepared to demonstrate that those who show resentment are justified in doing so.[64] Following Gabriele Taylor, I would say that the justified anger that constitutes my resentment is indeed justified if the following conditions are met:

1. The object of my anger must exist.
2. The wrong I believe myself to be suffering really must be a wrong and not just irrationally seen as such. And this involves:
3. I must have a well-founded notion of what is due to me, or due to

people in general, for otherwise it will not be the case that what I regard as undeserved or unfair harm was really undeserved.
4. I must have reason to believe that the agent I hold responsible is capable of recognizing what is due to me or to others, either on the grounds that the individual belongs to a class of beings, members of which are expected to conform to certain standards, or because, in this particular situation, it is natural or proper to make certain demands of that particular agent.
5. For the sake of completeness, we should add that, if my anger *with* X is to be justified, then it must be X and no one else who brought about the harm I suffered.[65]

Notice that the second through the fourth conditions all involve appraisals of one kind or another. The third condition, in particular, accounts for the idea that resentment is essentially tied up with self-respect, for what makes resentment *justified* anger is the emotional protest against not receiving what is our due. On the other hand, *unjustified* anger may result from our having an inflated or distorted view of what is our due.

On the basis of these various features of resentment, we can now see with even greater clarity that a lack of resentment on this or that occasion is evidence of a moral failing. Furthermore, different kinds of failings may be involved, depending on the different ways of looking at a situation. We can, for instance, not resent our neighbor, though we realize that she is trying to insult us. Here, our moral failing may be due to the fact that we take a very low view of her. In this case, our lack of resentment shows up as a failing because we should not view people with such little regard. Quite to the contrary, it seems entirely appropriate that we should feel resentment.[66]

We may also fail to experience resentment for reasons having to do not with arrogance, but with an excess of humility. In Jane Austen's *Emma*, for instance, Emma Woodhouse thinks that Miss Campbell should have felt resentment when her fiance preferred Jane Fairfax's inferior piano playing to her own. Frank Churchill remarks,

> It was not very flattering to Miss Campbell; but she really did not seem to feel it.

Emma then replies,

> So much the better—or so much the worse—I do not know which. It may be sweetness or it may be stupidity in her—quickness of friendship or dullness of feeling.[67]

Unlike the previous case, Miss Campbell's lack of resentment is a result of her failing to see that what has been said is hurtful to her. In both cases, however, the moral failing that the lack of resentment points to is the absence of a well-founded notion of our own and others' moral due.

Interestingly enough, Nietzsche has argued that a truly strong person (*Übermensch*) will not feel resentment, since resentment is a sign of weakness. If we feel physically, psychologically, or politically weak, we will feel threatened by those perceived as stronger. If we are injured by these stronger persons, our weakness will prevent us from venting our anger in the form of retaliation. Rather than venting our anger through action, or even perhaps feeling able to do so but choosing not to, we allow our perceived helplessness to transform our anger into brooding resentment. Such resentment, Nietzche thinks, poisons the soul and is both ugly and harmful. Because of this, he maintains that it is better to look away.[68]

It is also interesting to note that Murphy is sympathetic to this account of resentment, despite his claim that resentment is essentially linked with self-respect. "If one is certain of the value of one's self, it will not truly be threatened by attack from another and will not stand in need of defense."[69] However, he goes on to say that, since we are never quite sure of such matters, some weakness is always inevitable.

Murphy quotes favorably from David Hume, who wrote that "men always consider the sentiments of others in their judgments of themselves"[70] and hence are never so strong as to be indifferent to all such attacks.[71]

Certainly, if we take the Übermensch to be the paradigm of the moral personality, then resentment will never be justified, because other people simply do not matter. We in the above example who do not resent our neighbor's attempts to insult us are rather like the Übermensch in this way. However (happily), Murphy is correct in pointing out that in reality we are never so strong as to be completely indifferent to attacks on our self-esteem. Bernard Boxhill has argued similarly in a slightly different context:

> A person with self-respect may lose it. He may not be confident of always having it. He may not even be sure that he really has it. But if he does have self-respect, he will never be unconcerned about the question of self-respect. Necessarily, he will want to retain it. But no one will be satisfied that he has something unless he knows that he has it. Hence, the self-respecting person wants to know that he is self-respecting.[72]

To this I might add that the Übermensch's emotional reaction (or lack thereof) to personal injury is not justified, since it rests on a mistaken belief about moral desert. By this, I mean that all persons have value as ends-in-themselves.

There are, to be sure, other views about what constitutes a person's moral worth. Thomas Hobbes, for instance, says at one point that a person's value is merely instrumental. Hobbes writes, "The value, or worth, of a man is, as of all other things, his price; that is to say, so much as would be given for the use of his power."[73] So, too, some critics charge utilitarians with holding the view that a person's moral worth is determined solely on the basis of her potential contribution to the common good.[74] But rather than argue the point, I shall simply assume the truth of the Kantian view of moral worth, which sees persons as having value in and of themselves as members in a kingdom of ends.

Is Resentment a Virtue?

Since I have argued that we ought to feel resentment against those who have injured us, it is natural to conclude that a disposition to resent when resentment is warranted is a desirable trait and should be counted among our list of virtues. While I do draw this inference, a supporting argument is nonetheless needed. This is because, first, a disposition to resent is often thought of as a vice, if anything, and in any event is not ordinarily listed among the beneficial character traits we are exhorted to possess; and, second, it is simply not true that desirable traits are, eo ipso, virtuous traits. Memory, for instance, is a desirable trait; yet, hardly anyone would argue that memory is a virtue.

With respect to the first reason for a supporting argument, I have already indicated why I think that resentment's bad reputation is undeserved. It is, as I have argued, not resentment per se that is morally suspect, but resentment that is in excess, misplaced, or vindictive. Thus, we need no longer be concerned with the popular view, which construes resentment to be undesirable. It is to the second reason, then, that we must direct our attention.

To determine if a disposition to resent when resentment is warranted should be counted on the list of virtuous traits, we must identify precisely those features that virtues are thought to possess. While there is considerable debate over what constitutes virtue,[75] for Philippa Foot, at least, virtues are characterized by the following properties:

(1) They are beneficial traits, benefiting the owner as well as others concerned; (2) they "belong to the will"; and (3) they are corrective, in the sense that they stand at a point where there is some temptation to be resisted or some deficiency of motivation to be made good.[76] Assuming the adequacy of Foot's analysis, we are in a position to determine if (justified) resentment falls within its scope.

With respect to the first property, I have already shown that resentment is a beneficial character trait. Not to feel resentment when resentment is warranted is to display a lack of self-respect. Thus, since it is better to be self-respectful than it is to be servile, the possession of this quality is beneficial to its owner, and it is also beneficial to others concerned. Think here of Tolstoy's famous comment that there would not be any wars if everyone insisted on defending their own rights.[77]

With respect to the second property, we must first clarify what Foot means when she says that virtues "belong to the will." For reasons that go beyond the scope of this discussion, Foot uses the term "will" to include not only what is subject to volitional control but also what is wished for, as well as what is sought.[78] Given this broad construction of the concept of will, it follows that resentment belongs to the will for the following reason: A person who is disposed toward resentment is, as I have urged, interested in affirming respect for herself as well as such respect for others as is required by morality. Foot contends that we judge people not solely by their actions, but also by their desires and attitudes. What follows from this is that a disposition to resent when resentment is warranted satisfies the second property, insofar as it expresses a person's concern with respect for self and others.

Finally, with respect to the third property, it is easy to see how resentment would be "corrective." Not to feel resentment when resentment is warranted is, as we have seen, a sign that one does not think one has rights or that one does not take one's rights seriously. But since we do have rights and we should take them seriously, a character trait that motivates us to do this is to that extent corrective. From this, it follows that resentment is corrective in the specified sense.

Given Foot's analysis of what constitutes a virtue, then, a disposition to resent when resentment is warranted may be counted as a virtue. Needless to say, the disposition I have described should not be confused with the disposition to resent as it is ordinarily understood. When we think, for instance, of the resentful personality, what ordinarily comes to mind is a person who is disposed to resent no matter what the occasion. That, however, is hardly a virtue and is not the disposition to which I have been referring.

Again, objections could be raised against the view I have advanced. Elizabeth Beardsley, for one, does not seem to think that resentment (even of the justifiable variety) is a virtue, although she does admit that it is a desirable trait. Apparently, Beardsley comes to this conclusion believing that resentment is linked to "self-love."

> I believe that though resentment is sometimes justified . . . a capacity for resentment is not a moral virtue. A capacity for moral indignation is a desirable trait, and when it is a question of moral indignation on behalf of another, the capacity for adopting this attitude is a moral virtue. But resentment is moral indignation on behalf of oneself. A capacity for resentment is a desirable trait. We admire those who "stand up for their rights," and to refuse to become indignant on one's own behalf would be to fail to treat humanity in one's own person in the same way as humanity in the person of another. Therefore, to repress resentment is wrong. But capacity for resentment is linked to self-love.[79]

I have two responses to Beardsley's argument. The first concerns her tacit assumption that a trait linked to self-love precludes us from counting that trait as a virtue. If, by "self-love," Beardsley means *self-respect*, then I do not at all understand why the disposition to resent when resentment is warranted is not a virtue, unless it could be shown that duties to the self do not exist. If, however, we are prepared to include duties to the self as part of our moral vocabulary, and if the duty to respect ourselves falls within its purview, then the fact that resentment is linked to self-respect is hardly disturbing. As I see it, our moral vocabulary does admit of duties to the self, and Beardsley provides no argument to the contrary.

Furthermore—and this is my second point—if, by "self-love," what Beardsley means is that resentment is a partially *selfish* attitude, then this too is hardly disturbing. Earlier, we saw that resentment, while *essentially* linked with egoistical concerns, is also linked with concern for others. Recall how in expressing resentment we show our respect for the one who has injured us. Thus, even if Beardsley is correct in arguing that resentment is a selfish attitude, it is not *purely* selfish.

In conclusion, what I have endeavored to show throughout this chapter is that resentment has value as a response to moral injury, despite the popular view that would seem to be otherwise. In the final analysis, this should not be surprising, since Aristotle—the father of virtue theory—also appears to have held this view. At least something of this sort seems implicit in his discussion of *epiekia*, where he contrasts proper with improper anger.[80] In the spirit of Aristotle, we can say with confidence that resentment is the mean between the extremes of abject servitude and excessive anger.

5

The Ethics of Forgiveness

In the previous chapter, I argued that resentment is the morally proper response to injury—that a self-respecting person is open to moral criticism if she fails to resent those who have wronged her. Given this thesis, it follows that, all things being equal, we ought not to forgive those who have injured us.

Despite the powerful tradition that says one is never wrong to forgive and perhaps is always wrong not to do so, I think we can accept the above conclusion given what I have said about the propriety of resentment. Certainly, again using Jeffrie Murphy's examples as in Chapter 4, a former inmate of a concentration camp ought not to forgive his camp commandant for inflicting what injuries he did; certainly, American soldiers ought not to forgive those who exposed them to radiation poisoning.[1] Hard feelings in these cases are not only natural but are called for as expressions of aversion to mistreatment. Since, as we had noted, these are model cases of justified anger, in order to argue against the propriety of forgiveness we must do so against the backdrop of these types of cases.

Nevertheless, the conclusion is counterintuitive. What accounts for this, I believe, is the ceteris paribus clause. Whether one should or should not forgive often depends on the relationship of the parties, the culpability of the wrongdoer, the magnitude of the wrong, and so forth. But in saying this, we already have a clue as to why it is thought that forgiveness is proper and even demanded. Often, if not always, we forgive *for a reason*. On those occasions when we harbor resentment, it is not uncommon to ask, "Why *should* I forgive?"—with hard emphasis on the "should." Unless I am mistaken, what we look for in forgiving is a reason to forgive which would negate the reason for the victim's anger. In asking "Why *should* I forgive?" we are presupposing that we should *not* forgive in the absence of a reason to the contrary.

The question we need to ask here is, what kind of reason makes forgiveness appropriate? When is it that we may change our attitude from resentment to forgiveness without risking moral reproval? If, as I have urged, resentment is associated with self-respect, then it would appear that forgiveness is appropriate when tendered for a reason that *preserves* self-respect. In other words, an appropriate reason would be one that negates the justifiability of the injured party's resentment. As I shall argue below, the only reason that would serve this function is that the wrongdoer has repented the wrong she has done.

To be sure, we often forgive for reasons other than repentance. We forgive, for instance, for "old times' sake," because the wrongdoer has meant well, has suffered enough, and so on. Murphy, for one, would countenance any reason as being relevant to forgiveness so long as such reason is *consistent* with self-respect.[2] However, as I shall argue later in the chapter, consistency with self-respect is too weak a criterion. For now, suffice it to say that, for forgiveness to be appropriate, it must reflect the demand that wrongdoers "pay" for the wrongs they have done, and it cannot rest on uncertainty about one's own rights or on fears about defending them.[3] I turn, then, to an analysis of repentance and why it is appropriate as a reason to forgive.

Repentance

As I see it, the only acceptable reason to forgive a wrongdoer is that the wrongdoer has repented the wrong she did—has had a change of heart (*metanoia*)[4] with respect to her wrongful action. By repenting, the wrongdoer repudiates the wrong that she did and vows not to repeat such wrongdoing again. This being so, we are then able to join her in resenting the very act from which she now stands separated, without compromising our self-respect.[5] In the absence of repentance, forgiveness amounts to little more than condonation of wrongdoing.

To see this is so, we must first explain what is meant by "repentance." As I see it, repentance is comprised of two distinct elements. The first is regret—or remorse—over the past misdeed. In the classic description, the repentant wrongdoer is contrite, or "bruised in the heart." The second element is the promise made to refrain from repeating the misdeed in question (or, for that matter, any misdeed at all). Thus, repentance, as I understand it, has both an emotional and volitional component. The emotional component is the regret felt over the past misdeed, and the volitional component is the promise to refrain from further misconduct. Needless to say, there is a sincerity condition attached to both of these: The regret must be genuine, and the promise sincere.

Often, the promise to refrain from further misconduct is a natural concomitant of genuine regret. It is not, however, an inevitable one. One can, for instance, genuinely regret not having finished high school, with no intention of doing so later. What this suggests is that there are different kinds of regret, not all of which are relevant to our conception of repentance. What is needed, then, is a notion of regret that is related to the promise in the sense of providing a motive to reform. However, we also need a notion of regret that is morally related to the promise as well. As I shall argue below, even where the regret works to inspire the relevant promise, it may do so for reasons inappropriate to forgiveness.

In an interesting paper on regret and forgiveness,[6] Martin Golding has identified three types of regret that are unusually helpful for the present analysis.[7] The first type of regret, which Golding refers to as "intellectual regret"[8] (I-regret hereinafter), is the type of regret that "arises from a recognition of having misjudged the facts as they were, of having miscalculated the future, or from the calculation in itself."[9] This type of regret issues, for example, from one who has lent a needy person a sum of money, only to see that person buy cocaine instead of food. It is this type of regret that ostensibly issues from the person who failed to finish high school.

For several reasons, I-regret is too weak to be of use for our conception of repentance. First, this type of regret does not contain within it the recognition that what was done was morally wrong. This is because either what was done was *not* morally wrong (such as failing to finish high school), or—where what was done *was* morally wrong—there is no *recognition* of the moral wrong. As an example of this latter, Golding provides the following:

> At the trials of the Nazi officers after the war, some of the men in the dock expressed regret over what they had done and asked forgiveness from the relatives of the victims. But suppose Hitler had won the war? Would they have been regretful? Did they regret this misdeed *because* Hitler lost?[10]

Assuming the answer is yes to this question, it is clear why such regret is too weak to be of use for our conception of repentance. Such regret is too weak not because it is insincere, but because—even if sincere—it is not for the crimes committed. Because of this, I-regret is not likely to inspire a promise to reform and thus fails to satisfy the motivational criterion.

Second, I-regret is too weak for our conception of repentance because, even if it could inspire a promise to reform, this would not be for reasons that are morally relevant. Ostensibly, the one who has so promised to change behavior makes such a promise only because of the regretted miscalculation. Had the facts been otherwise, such a promise would have been unlikely. Thus, in addition to being motivationally unrelated to the promise to change, I-regret is morally unrelated to the promise as well; and this latter is true even in those cases where the regret may work to inspire the promise.

The second type of regret, which Golding refers to as "moral regret"[11] (M-regret), issues from the recognition that one has done wrong but fails to include the recognition that one has wronged *someone in particular*. One may, for instance, regret having cheated on one's income tax returns, realize that what was done was wrong, but be blind to the fact that someone was injured in a discernible way.

Unlike I-regret, M-regret may very well inspire a promise to change, since there is within it recognition of wrongdoing. Because of this, M-regret satisfies our motivational criterion. To see this, recall that, in resenting a wrongdoer, what we emotionally convey is that we respect ourselves, others, and the normative order. M-regret, however, speaks only to the normative order. It does not address the fact that a particular person has been morally injured. A person who experiences M-regret is, by definition, oblivious to having wronged someone in particular. This being so, any promise to change that might be forthcoming is a promise to refrain from wrongful actions *in general*. It would not be a promise made to the victim *in particular*. Consequently, M-regret is morally irrelevant to repentance, because there is no recognition of having wronged someone else.

This brings us to the third and most important type of regret, which Golding refers to as "other-oriented regret"[12] (O-regret). O-regret issues from the recognition of wrongdoing that has resulted in an injury to someone in particular. It is, as Golding rightfully points out, the type of regret that one may properly consider when entertaining forgiveness. The reason for this is as follows: In expressing O-regret, a wrongdoer acknowledges not only that she has done wrong, but that she has wronged someone in particular. Thus, not only is O-regret likely to inspire a promise to change, but the promise is actually made to the victim in question. Because of this, O-regret satisfies both the motivational and moral criteria of repentance.

At this point, the question may be raised as to whether there is any real difference between the promise that issues from M-regret and the promise that issues from O-regret. Logically, there may not be much difference. To see this, consider the following two cases, which are designed to illustrate the promises that issue from M-regret and O-regret, respectively:

Case 1: Smith does something wrong and, as a result, injures Jones. Smith, mindful of doing wrong *but not of wronging Jones*, M-regrets her action and vows not to repeat such action again.

Case 2: Smith does something wrong and, as a result, injures Jones. Smith, mindful of doing wrong *and of wronging Jones*, O-regrets her action and vows not to wrong Jones in this way again.

Note the essential difference between the two promises: In Case 1, it is *implicit* in Smith's promise not to repeat such action again that Smith intends not to wrong Jones again. In Case 2, Smith makes *explicit* that she will not wrong Jones again. Since, as a result of either promise, Jones will be spared Smith's wrongful behavior, why should the promise made in Case 2 be any more relevant than the promise in Case 1?

To answer this question, it will help to recall that forgiveness is essentially a personal response to moral injury; it is not a response to wrongdoing per se. This being so, it follows that, whatever counts as a reason to forgive, such reason should reflect the fact that a particular victim has been morally injured. Since, as I have urged, repentance is such a reason, the regret and promise that are constituents thereof should be of a kind that is eminently personal. Just as a lover is not moved by her beloved's declarations that he loves all humankind (thereby implying that he loves her as well), so, too, the victim of an injury is not moved by the wrongdoer's promise to refrain from further wrongs (thereby implying that she will not commit a wrong against the victim as well).[13] On the other hand, if the wrongdoer promises not to commit *only* the wrong that occasioned the injury, the promise made will hardly be adequate. Before we forgive, we want some strong assurances of change, and not only that the wrongdoer will not injure us in the same way again. Otherwise put, if, when we resent a wrongdoer, we are conveying to her that we respect ourselves, others, and the moral law, then we want the kind of promise that addresses all three of these. At a minimum, we want the wrongdoer to promise not to repeat the misdeed that occasioned the injury, and we want this promise to be made explicit to us; but we also want the wrongdoer to promise to refrain from all misdeeds to us, owing to respect for the moral law. Without this latter, the wrongdoer's promise is likely to be specious. Thus, O-regret and the promise not to repeat the particular action that occasioned the injury are necessary, but not always sufficient, conditions of the kind of repentance that makes forgiveness acceptable.

To summarize, I have construed repentance to consist of a certain type of regret (O-regret) and a promise not to repeat at least the misdeed that occasioned the victim's resentment. I have also suggested that repentance is uniquely applicable as a reason to forgive. So far only hinting at why this is so, I have yet to put forward a developed argument. However, before I do that, it is important to offer a defense of repentance against those who see it as morally worthless.

Despite its relevance to the issue of forgiveness, repentance has suffered a bad reputation. In addition to being a backward-looking emotion and thus denounced by utilitarians, some see in repentance a form of self-deception. It has been said, for instance, that repentance consists in our setting ourselves against a past reality and absurdly attempting to efface that reality from the world. It has also been said that in repenting our misdeeds we confuse our memory image of the deed with the deed itself, and that it is to this image that the remorse we feel is directed. This is the way Nietzsche, for one, sought to explain away repentance as a form of self-deception. The repentant wrongdoer cannot endure the "image of his deed" and "calumniates" the deed through this "image." For Nietzsche, "bad conscience" is an historical phenomenon that arose when passions of hate, revenge, cruelty, and spite—which were once allowed free play—came to be damned by the State and thereupon turned for their satisfaction against those who felt them.[14]

Perhaps, however, the most biting indictment of repentance comes from Spinoza. When people make mistakes, Spinoza says,

> one might expect gnawings of conscience and repentance to help bring them on the right path, and might thereupon conclude (as everyone does conclude) that these affections are good things. Yet when we look at the matter closely, we shall find that not only are they not good, but on the contrary deleterious and evil passions. For it is manifest that we can always get along better by reason and love of truth than by the worry of

> conscience and remorse. Harmful are these and evil, inasmuch as they form a particular kind of sadness; and the disadvantages of sadness I have already proved, and shown that we should strive to keep it from our life. Just so we should endeavor, since uneasiness of conscience and remorse are of this kind of complexion, to flee and shun these states of mind.[15]

William James echoes these thoughts when he writes that "evil is a disease; and worry over disease is itself an additional form of disease. . . . The best repentance is to up and act for righteousness, and to forget that you ever had relations with sin."[16]

As I see it, these comments are directed not at repentance as I have construed it, but at the regret that is a constituent thereof. Were it not for the promise that issues from regret, much of this criticism would have some validity. Also, I might add, the regret that is the target of the above criticism is regret that is of a pathological nature. Certainly, regret *can* be a "spiritual deadweight," "form of self-deception," "kind of disease," but the point is that it *need not be*. Regret is rational and productive when what issues from it is the kind of promise of which I have been speaking.

Notwithstanding my defense of regret, however, there is some merit to the above criticism. Why, it may be asked, should a wrongdoer regret her behavior *and* promise not to repeat it when the relevant promise seems more than sufficient? Is not this promise a sufficient reason to tender forgiveness? What does regret add to our conception of repentance that the relevant promise does not accomplish alone? To answer this question, it will help to remember that being moral is not just a matter of assenting to principles, but a matter of internalizing these principles as well. Being moral is a matter of having moral emotions such as guilt and regret at one's own misconduct. This is why, for instance, we admire people who regret their wrongdoing and castigate people who do not. In the words of Jeffrie Murphy, "morality . . . is not simply something to be believed; it is something to be *cared* about."[17]

Forgiving Repentant Wrongdoers

Now that I have explained what I mean by repentance, and have defended it against those who see it as worthless, it is time to substantiate my claim that repentance is relevant as a reason to forgive. Earlier, I mentioned that the repentant wrongdoer repudiates her deed and refuses to identify with the person she was who committed it. What this suggests is that, by repenting, the wrongdoer can in some sense become a new person; that by repenting her deed, the person she was who committed the wrong is nothing more than a metaphysical shadow. Should this be the case, we would then be able to join the wrongdoer in resenting the person from whom she now stands detached. The question that needs to be asked is, how and in what sense can repentance effectuate such a moral rebirth?

The idea that repentance can transform an old person into a new one was suggested by Kant in his *Religion within the Limits of Reason Alone*.[18] In this book, where he addresses the question of forgiveness, Kant is concerned with sustaining our hope in a forgiveness that would be consistent with his view that moral wrong ought always to be punished. Kant's problem was this: Given his conception of freedom, we are always responsible for what wrongs we commit. Even God—a Divine Judge against whose law we transgress—cannot, in his capacity as Judge, change His mind about our moral deserts. We will always receive our just deserts with or without our prayers. However, Kant felt that, by repenting, we are able to effect what might be called a new birth, with the result that the sinful person we once were will be punished while the new person we become will not.[19]

This interpretation of the mystery of atonement is a plausible solution, at least as it relates to guilt deriving from an evil disposition. It is not, however, without its problems. Why, we may ask, should a person receive absolution from a Divine Judge who is not disposed to offer it—committed, as He is, to the moral law? John Silber has argued, "If Kant had consistently held to his theory of unqualified freedom he would have followed the line of argument taken by Ivan Karamazov. . . . Forgiveness, as Ivan observed following Kantian principles, is itself a violation of the moral law."[20]

There are also problems with Kant's concept of personal identity transformation—problems that are far too complex to be dealt with here. However, the main point Kant wishes to advance is that the difference between a person with an evil disposition and a person with a good one is so great that the new person, structured as she is by a good disposition, is justified in denying identity with the old one. This follows from the fact that, according to Kant, a person's disposition is itself the basis for moral self-identity.[21]

As mentioned above, this interpretation of the mystery of atonement is a plausible solution to the problem of forgiveness as an ethical act. If, by repenting, a wrongdoer can deny identity with the person she was who committed the wrong, we can forgive that person and at the same time maintain our self-respect. However, because of the problems with this rebirth position, it creates more difficulties than it ostensibly cures. Furthermore, even if we could respond to these troubles, Kant's solution proves more than is needed. Rather than arguing that repentance serves to change one's moral identity from sinner to saint, a more innocuous approach is to argue that repentance cures the single defect that led to the misdeed. Such an approach is suggested by Norvin Richards in his article "Forgiveness."[22]

Far from seeing repentance as transforming us from one kind of person into another, Richards sees repentance as accomplishing a more modest task. To begin with, Richards sees repentance not only as including negative feelings about one's prior misconduct, but as having these feelings as part of a change in one's moral views. Thus, according to Richards, the repentant wrongdoer acquires a new moral principle when she realizes that her old ones are morally bad. When this occurs, the wrongdoer realizes that her old principles were partly responsible for her behaving immorally. For instance, the wrongdoer may have shouted at her secretary, in part because she thought there is nothing wrong in shouting at secretaries. However, in repenting, the wrongdoer realizes that such behavior is wrong; this change in her views is a change in something that was responsible for the wrong. It is not, however, a change in the person considered as a whole.[23] "Her repentance is . . . like repairing that part of a house which contributed to the accident. The child took a nasty fall right here, in part because the steps were uneven, but now I have fixed them. . . . Despite the change, this is still the house where the child fell."[24] To continue the metaphor, such repentance is acceptable provided the house is otherwise sound: The wrongdoer's overall respect for the moral law is at issue along with regret for the particular act, as mentioned earlier.

As I see it, Richards's analysis is preferable to Kant's. Rather than saying that repentance transforms an individual from one kind of person into another—thereby creating problems of personal identity—Richards's analysis avoids such problems, while providing us with a reason we may use to forgive. Forgiveness, as mentioned at the very start of this book, is always *of* an offender *for* an offense. This being so, we would be asking too much if we asked of a wrongdoer that she repent her evil ways, where this would include *all* her evil ways. All things being equal, it is sufficient that she regret her behavior and vow not to repeat it toward us again. Of course, if the wrongdoer has repeatedly committed acts that have injured us, we may require her repentance in the Kantian sense. But to the extent that we are forgiving for one offense only, it will suffice that the wrongdoer repent only that offense.

Given this analysis, it is possible to say that, when a wrongdoer repents, she is no longer the person she was who committed the wrong, in the limited sense that the new person subscribes to a moral principle that the old person does not (or manifests a new determination to abide by an old principle). Through the act of repentance, the reformed individual denies identity with the wrongdoer, and the reason for resentment no longer obtains. Consequently, it is now possible to tender forgiveness without sacrificing self-respect.

What follows from this is that, while we can forgive a person in the absence of repentance, we ought not to do so if our forgiveness is to be morally respectable. Susan Jacoby has written,

> Without contrition on the part of the offender, forgiveness is simply a state of mind—a condition that may be emotionally . . . meaningful to the one who forgives but has no significance as a social or moral bond, as a medium for restoring civilized relations between the injured and the injurer.[25]

And again:

> The absolute importance of reciprocity is apparent in considering the process of reconciliation as it applies to every offense from the most mundane violation of domestic order to the most grievous crimes against humanity. In our private lives, we are all familiar with the difference between a friend or lover who simply says "I'm sorry you're hurt," and the one who says, "What I did was wrong; you have every right to be hurt and I'm sorry." The former personality somehow manages to place the entire burden of forgiveness on the one who has already been hurt.[26]

Note Jacoby's allusion to the act of apologizing. Given what I have said about the desirability of repentance, it follows—not surprisingly—that certain actions have value as *expressions* of repentance. Here, as was said about resentment in Chapter 4, it is difficult to drive an impenetrable wedge between how we feel and how we behave. There is a sense in which one cannot be said to have repented at all in the absence of characteristic behavior. Thus, once again, we may say that repentance has both an internal and external aspect about it; the internal aspect being the emotional change that the wrongdoer has experienced, and the external aspect to be discussed below.

As Jacoby suggests, the characteristic way of expressing repentance is in the form of an apology. By apologizing, the wrongdoer makes it known that she need no longer be the object of her victim's resentment. More precisely, in expressing her repentance (apologizing) of an act A to a victim V, an agent X represents as true the following statements:

(1) X did A;
(2) A was wrong;
(3) X was responsible for doing A;
(4) V was personally injured by X's doing A;
(5) V resented being injured by X's doing A;
(6) X regrets doing A;
(7) X vows not to commit A against V again;

and, for the sake of completeness:

(8) X has respect for the rules of morality, which mandate that we accord moral agents the respect they deserve.[27]

There are several points to be made about the above. First, note how statements (1) through (4) plus (8) are identical to those statements made by a victim who expresses *resentment* (except for the subject of (8), the person doing the representing).[28] This should not surprise us, given my thesis that repentance is appropriate as a reason to forgive. It is precisely because the wrongdoer realizes the reason for the victim's anger—and responds to that reason in a relevant way—that repentance has value as a reason to forgive. These statements having been represented, the attitude of resentment is no longer necessary. A victim need no longer protest her having been injured, since the justifiability of her resentment has now been negated.

To see this more clearly, recall that expressions of resentment are demonstrations of a complex of beliefs, feelings, and attitudes that are appropriate to members of the moral community; they constitute a form of protest against being treated unjustly. However, because of repentance, we no longer have reason to continue the protest. Otherwise stated, by regretting her misdeed (statement (6) of repentance) and vowing not to commit it again (statement (7) of repentance), the wrongdoer tacitly affirms that the victim has rights (statement (5) of resentment). Thus, by expressing repentance, we may say that the wrongdoer would herself have resented her own moral injury had she been the one who was the victim of her injury.

There are two other points to be discussed about the representations made in an expression of repentance. First, note that I have used "X" to represent the wrongdoer. I could easily have used "S" (previously used to represent the speaker of "I forgive you"), since an expression of repentance that constitutes an apology is a performative utterance as understood by John L. Austin.[29] Second, note that I have not qualified the regret felt in statement (6). That this is O-regret follows from statements (1) through (5).

Having analyzed what it means to feel and express repentance, we now have the conceptual material needed to schematize an account of forgiveness that is morally respectable. Assuming an ordinary, interpersonal situation in which an agent X commits an act A that injures a victim V, V would resent this act and express her resentment, representing as true the following statements:

(1) X did A;
(2) A was wrong;
(3) X was responsible for doing A;
(4) V was personally injured by X's doing A;
(5) V has rights that V herself respects;
(6) X has rights that ought to be respected; and
(7) V has respect for the rules of morality, which mandate that we accord moral agents the respect they deserve.

On learning of V's resentment, X would then repent and express her repentance (apologize), representing these statements:

(1) X did A;
(2) A was wrong;
(3) X was responsible for doing A;
(4) V was personally injured by X's doing A;
(5) V resented being injured by X's doing A;
(6) X regrets doing A;
(7) X vows not to commit A against V again; and
(8) X has respect for the rules of morality, which mandate that we accord moral agents the respect they deserve.

On learning of X's repentance, V would then express her forgiveness, representing these statements:

(1) X did A;
(2) A was wrong;

(3) X was responsible for doing A;
(4) V was personally injured by X's doing A;
(5) V resented being injured by X's doing A; and
(6) V has overcome her resentment for X's doing A, or is at least willing to try to overcome it, since X has repented her wrongful behavior.

As I see it, this is an analytical picture of how it looks to tender forgiveness in a way that is morally respectable. My next task is to substantiate the claim that repentance is *uniquely* appropriate as a reason to forgive. Before I do that, I must point out that, from what has been said thus far, the conclusion has been reached that forgiveness is *permissible* when a wrongdoer repents—that we cannot be accused of servility when we give our forgiveness to a repentant wrongdoer. Because the reason for our resentment is negated by repentance, it is possible to forgive and maintain self-respect. There is, however, more to be said. For it is one thing to say that one does not act immorally when one tenders forgiveness to a repentant wrongdoer (which conclusion is what has been reached), and it is another to say that forgiveness has positive moral value. We need to show not only that one does nothing wrong in tendering forgiveness, but that there are times when forgiveness is morally called for.

To begin with, the fact that a wrongdoer repents does not mean the wrongdoer has a right to be forgiven. The wrongdoer's repentance means only that the victim may forgive and maintain self-respect. Were this not true, then, as Aurel Kolnai has pointed out, the following paradox would emerge: If we forgive a wrongdoer in the absence of repentance, the forgiveness collapses into condonation. However, it is wrong to condone wrongful behavior, while it is not wrong to tender forgiveness. Furthermore, if the wrongdoer were then to repent, there would be nothing to forgive. Thus, the forgiveness is either unjustified or pointless.[30]

The existence of this paradox is enough to show that forgiveness is not earned by the act of repentance. As P. Twambley has put it, "*metanoia* is a highly relevant factor in deciding whether to *tender* forgiveness,"[31] but its presence does not mean that a wrongdoer *earns* it. Otherwise—as Herbert Fingarette quips—by the act of repentance, "beggar would be chooser."[32] While we do sometimes say that a wrongdoer "owes" her victim an apology (having put herself in "debt" to the victim), to take this literally would mean that the "debt" is satisfied when the wrongdoer repents. But then, once more, forgiveness would be pointless.

We see, then, that repentance does not earn a victim's forgiveness, which means forgiveness is at the victim's discretion. Nevertheless, we do not think well of a person who fails to forgive a repentant wrongdoer. So the question remains: How can the mere permissibility of forgiveness be reconciled with our tendency to censure some unforgiving persons?

To answer this question, it will help if we attend to the particular times when we tend to censure the withholding of forgiveness. Actually—unless I am mistaken—it is not as though we censure the withholding of forgiveness on this or that occasion; rather, we censure people who are in the habit of withholding forgiveness generally. Anthony Trollope, for one, understood this well when, in *Orley Farm*, he describes Sir Joseph Mason as "a bad man in that he could *never* . . . forgive."[33] As Murphy has put it, "part of what makes forgiveness a virtue is the tendency to forgive when forgiveness is appropriate."[34] In this sense, forgiveness may be thought of as belonging to the class of what Kant called "imperfect duties"—that is, duties that admit of exceptions in the interest of inclination.[35] Thus, while I do no wrong if I withhold forgiveness from *one* who has injured me, it does not follow that I do no wrong if I withhold forgiveness from *all* who have injured me. To again quote Murphy: "Just as charity requires that I sometimes ought to assist those having no right to my assistance, so does forgiveness require that I sometimes ought to forgive those having no right to my forgiveness."[36] With respect to any particular injury, however, no one has a *right* to my forgiveness. What John Rawls has said about envy, therefore, applies to forgiveness—namely, that "sometimes the circumstances evoking envy are so compelling that, given human beings as they are, no one can reasonably be asked to overcome his rancorous feelings."[37]

The distinction between withholding forgiveness on particular occasions and withholding forgiveness as a matter of habit is an important distinction to keep in mind. Consider, for instance, what Hannah Arendt has to say about the withholding of forgiveness from the wrongdoer's perspective:

> Without being forgiven, released from the consequences of what we have done, our capacity to act would, as it were, be confined to one single deed from which we could never recover; we would remain the victims of its consequences forever, not unlike the sorcerer's apprentice who lacked the magic formula to break the spell.[38]

Clearly, Arendt is mistaken if she means this to apply to the withholding of forgiveness on a particular occasion. She is not mistaken if she means it to apply to the withholding of forgiveness as a matter of habit.

I might add here an interesting tidbit from Talmudic literature that serves to illustrate this point. Under Rabbinic law, on the eve of Yom Kippur, wrongdoers are obligated to ask forgiveness from those they have wronged. Should their request be denied, they are obligated to ask two more times, at which point, should their requests be denied, it is the victim—not the wrongdoer—who is morally to blame.[39] As I understand it, the point behind this Rabbinic law is precisely the one I have been making. Certainly, if the victim is permitted to withhold forgiveness, then it hardly makes a difference if she continues to withhold it. The number of times she is asked to forgive should hardly affect the justification behind her refusal. However, as far as I can tell, the point of this law is not to recognize a relevant difference in the number of times one is asked to forgive; rather, it is to discourage the habit of withholding forgiveness.

A further point I should hasten to add is that a disposition to forgive where forgiveness is permissible helps strengthen the bonds of moral community—the sharing of a common moral life based on respect for persons as ends-in-themselves. Repentance makes this possible since the repentant wrongdoer acknowledges her wrong and commits herself to not repeating it. In the absence of repentance, forgiveness could work to achieve this as well, of course. It would do so, however, at a cost to the victim.

The upshot, then, of what I have argued is this: It is morally wrong to forgive a wrongdoer unless the wrongdoer has repented her misdeed. In the absence of repentance, forgiveness betrays a lack of self-respect. Where, however, the wrongdoer repents, forgiving behavior is morally permissible. It is not morally required. No one has a right to be forgiven, imposing on others a perfect duty to forgive. Notwithstanding, if one never forgave repentant wrongdoers, one would be open to moral criticism. This is because a disposition to forgive when forgiveness is permissible is a virtuous trait and—being a virtue—requires that we ought to forgive on at least some occasions.

Forgiveness for Reasons Other Than Repentance

In putting forth repentance as a reason to forgive, I have thus far defended what may be thought of as a Kantian account of forgiving behavior. I began by arguing that—all things being equal—a self-respecting person ought to resent a wrongdoer's infliction of moral injury. From there, I proceeded to argue that, in those cases where a wrongdoer repents, an offer of forgiveness is morally permissible. This is because, by repenting, the wrongdoer acknowledges what wrong she committed and vows not to repeat such wrong again. The next question to ask, then, is whether this account presents itself as complete. As I shall argue below, the answer is yes.

Before I begin, it is important that I distinguish my position from Jeffrie Murphy's, who likewise has proffered a Kantian analysis. As Murphy sees it, forgiveness is permissible when tendered for a reason "not inconsistent with self-respect."[40] From his perspective, any reason whereby the wrongdoer can be separated from the wrong she committed meets this criterion and makes forgiveness permissible. He then goes on to list five ways in which this can occur. We can, he says, forgive a wrongdoer for any one or more of the following reasons:

1. She repented;
2. She meant well;
3. She has suffered enough;
4. She has undergone humiliation; or
5. For old times' sake.[41]

According to Murphy, each of these reasons allows us as the victim to draw a distinction between the immoral *act* and the immoral *agent*, so that forgiving the wrongdoer does not compromise our self-respect. We can then follow Augustine's counsel to "hate the sin but not the sinner."[42]

As I see it, there are two problems with Murphy's perspective. The first concerns his general claim that forgiveness is permissible so long as the victim can distinguish between act and agent. The second concerns the particular ways in which Murphy believes this can be done.

With respect to the first problem, Murphy is arguing that forgiveness is permissible so long as it is consistent with self-respect, and it is consistent with self-respect if the victim who forgives has reason to distinguish wrongdoer from wrong. As I see it, however, even if the victim can make such a distinction, it is not the *victim* who must make this distinction; rather, it is the *wrongdoer*. In other words, before we as the victim tender forgiveness, we want the wrongdoer to withdraw her endorsement of what she did. Then, first we can join her in condemning her evil deed, and then we can forgive. Murphy, on the other hand, is placing the onus of responsibility not on the wrongdoer—where it rightfully belongs—but on the victim who is deciding whether to forgive. This is at least true with regard to the four reasons Murphy lists other than repentance. Thus, even if a reason to forgive can be made "consistent" with self-respect, we want a stronger reason before we forgive. We want, I believe, a reason that will *cancel* our justified resentment. This reason, as I have argued, is the wrongdoer's repentance.

As far as the second problem is concerned, Murphy lists five ways in which a victim can distinguish wrongdoer from wrong. He does not, however, adequately explain why these should be counted as reasons to forgive. With respect to repentance, Murphy comes closest to what I have argued is an acceptable reason to forgive. But even here, he confuses repentance with *regret*, which is a constituent of repentance. Murphy says, "In having a sincere change of heart, he [the wrongdoer] is withdrawing his endorsement from his own past immoral behavior."[43] I have already argued early in the chapter that regret per se may not be relevant as a reason to forgive. We must also specify the *kind* of regret that the wrongdoer feels. Furthermore, even if the regret is of a relevant kind, the mere experience of it hardly suffices as a reason to forgive. Unless regret leads to a promise to refrain from further wrongdoing, why should a victim tender forgiveness? In the absence of such a promise, the victim is hardly assured that the wrongdoer will not repeat her immoral act. Thus, the best that can be said about Murphy's use of repentance is that it is the one of his five reasons for forgiveness that places the responsibility of wrongdoing on the wrongdoer herself.

With respect to the second of his reasons, Murphy is arguing that we may forgive a wrongdoer if the wrongdoer's misconduct was well intended.[44] He uses paternalism to illustrate this point. "A person," he says, "who interferes with my liberty for what he thinks is my own good is . . . acting wrongly; that is, he is interfering in my 'moral space' in a way he has no right to."[45] However, as Jean Hampton points out, if a victim believes that her wrongdoer thought she was doing what was *good* for the victim, the harm that was brought about can be said to be a mistake.[46] If this is the case, then the wrongdoer can be *excused* for what she has done. If the wrongdoer can be excused for what she has done, then the wrongdoer is not a wrongdoer at all. As Murphy himself has admitted, forgiveness and excuse are two distinct concepts.[47]

With respect to Murphy's third reason, the argument is made that we may forgive a wrongdoer who has already endured a great deal of suffering. Murphy then suggests that suffering can be redemptive. But once again, suffering per se is only redemptive if it is of a relevant kind. To use the example cited by Golding again, the Nazi soldiers may have suffered as a result of Hitler's having lost the war. But would they have suffered had he won? Clearly, a wrongdoer can endure a great deal of suffering due to her own wrongdoing; but unless she emerges a more decent individual, that suffering per se is an inadequate reason to forgive her.[48] The same may be said of Murphy's fourth reason: humiliation.

Finally, with respect to his fifth reason, Murphy is arguing that forgiveness is permissible for old times' sake. He writes, "When I forgive you for old times' sake, I forgive you for what you *once were*."[49] As I see it, however, what a person was is hardly relevant if what she is now is a wrongdoer. Furthermore, as Norvin Richards observes, "why should your having 'been a good and loyal friend to me in the past' be a reason to forgive you for wronging me, rather than something that deepens the hurt?"[50] Thus, in the final analysis, none of Murphy's reasons is without its problems, and his general criterion is too weak to be acceptable.

Having thus distinguished my position from that of Murphy, we may now consider whether my focus on repentance presents itself as the only good reason to forgive, or whether there are any other good reasons. As discussed below, we sometimes forgive for reasons that may be generally described as consequentialist in nature.

To begin with, we sometimes forgive so as to renew a relationship that was ruptured by a wrongdoer's immoral conduct. For example, an adulterous husband may seek forgiveness from his wife, and she may forgive him in the interests of marital harmony, to spare the children suffering, and so forth. However, while there is something to be said for these types of reasons, I would not countenance them as being morally relevant. The wife's interests do not reflect her having a sense of self-worth independent of the utilities that might accrue from her forgiveness. This is true even if, utilities aside, the wife's forgiveness issues from duties she may have to her children or husband. Furthermore, it is not even clear that the wife's forgiveness will result in positive utilities. In addition to losing the special contentment that comes from standing up for one's rights, her forgiveness may inspire further affairs. Having once been forgiven for reasons such as these, the adulterous husband may feel no compulsion to change, as he can always appeal to the same reasons. As Thomas Hill has pointed out, "When people refuse to press their rights, there are usually others who profit."[51]

There are other consequentialist reasons we sometimes offer in tendering forgiveness. There are times, for example, when we forgive so as to reform a wrongdoer. Here, as in the previous example, it is again not clear that the victim's forgiveness will have positive results. The wrongdoer may construe the victim's forgiveness as an act of arrogance. She may declare, "Who are *you* to forgive *me*!"—and be thereby disposed to even further misconduct. Certainly, not knowing beforehand the effects of forgiveness, we may find that forgiveness may actually increase wrongdoing. The main point here is that, even if such forgiveness proves beneficial, the benefits accrued do not negate the justifiability of the victim's resentment. I might add to this that, if the wrongdoer is forgiven to enable her to reform, she cannot see herself as in fact forgiven.

In addition to the above, we sometimes forgive for reasons having to do with our psychological well-being. Recently, psychologists have used forgiveness as a therapeutic means of enabling patients to release anger in a socially acceptable way. Richard Fitzgibbons explains,

> Forgiveness is a powerful therapeutic intervention which frees people from their anger and from the guilt which is often a result of unconscious anger. Forgiveness 1) helps individuals forget the painful experiences of their past and frees them from the subtle control of individuals and events of the past; 2) facilitates the reconciliation of relationships more than the expression of anger; and 3) decreases the likelihood that anger will be misdirected in later loving relationships and lessens the fear of being punished because of unconscious violent impulses.[52]

I have several responses to Dr. Fitzgibbons's comments. The first concerns his claim that forgiveness helps ease painful recollections and facilitates the reconciliation of relationships. While I do not deny that this may be true, it still does not follow that forgiveness is the appropriate response to these painful past occurrences. There simply are people whom it is better to resent than it is to forgive. Furthermore, while I do not deny that resentment can be distressing, can interfere with personal relationships, and can thoroughly dominate a person's life, I have taken pains to show that this need not be so. It is not an excess of resentment or misplaced resentment of which I have been speaking, but resentment that is felt in the right way, at the right time, before the right object.

Aside from these problems, the major criticism I have of Fitzgibbons is that the reasons he advances in defending forgiveness are largely irrelevant from the moral point of view. Certainly, forgiveness may accomplish all he suggests. However, in the absence of repentance, the reason that led to resentment in the first place does not get negated by therapeutic concerns. This, as we have seen, is what makes forgiveness *morally* permissible.

We see then that, whatever utilities accrue from forgiveness, none of them negates the reason for resentment. Nevertheless, as I suggested above, there is something attractive about the consequentialist line of thought. It is hard to dismiss as reasons to forgive such things as family harmony and psychological well-being. Because of this, it is important to be clear as to the precise reason why consequentialist reasons ought not to be countenanced.

As I see it, following Kant, consequentialist reasons to tender forgiveness are essentially practical, rather than moral. As Kant made clear, there is an important difference between engaging in behavior that is cost effective and engaging in behavior that is morally proper. Certainly, forgiveness for consequentialist reasons may result in positive utilities. It does not, however, follow that forgiveness for such reasons is the right path to follow. If, as I have argued, forgiveness is to be valued as a *moral* response, it must be tendered for a reason that is distinctively moral. It must reflect, that is, the idea that people have rights that ought to be respected. Thus, if the "ought" of forgiveness is to be anything more than a counsel of prudence, it must be directed at repentant wrongdoers. Otherwise, forgiving behavior is essentially no different from condonation of wrongdoing. This is true regardless of the positive utilities that result.

At this point, the objection may be raised that forgiveness can be justified notwithstanding the absence of repentance and even where forgiveness is not cost effective. Consider, for instance, someone who is obsessed with status, feels that the world has given her a raw deal, and harbors resentment against those she identifies as being in power. Suppose that, one day, this individual advances herself by engaging in wrongdoing and even feels vindicated that her aggressive self-concern is correct. The one whom she injures by committing the wrong might forgive her for what she did, regardless of the fact that she will not admit wrongdoing and that in no sense is she going to change.

It may be argued that the victim is justified in tendering forgiveness, since the forgiveness itself conveys a certain moral wisdom. The victim sees the wrongdoer as in some sense "fallen," as gripped by a self-diminishing passion, and as living out a certain kind of unhappiness. In other words, the victim understands the way in which it is not *the victim* at all who is the object of injury. Forgiveness here may be defended simply as the expression of a kind of insight into persons and their unhappiness. It is such forgiveness that may be attributed to Jesus and may be the kind of forgiveness the Crachits gave Scrooge.[53]

The thrust of this objection is that forgiveness can be justified in the absence of repentance and notwithstanding utilitarian concerns. This is because—in this case at least—forgiveness is itself the expression of a certain kind of moral wisdom. I do not deny that, in the case considered, the victim evinces a certain moral wisdom. What I do deny is that the wisdom evinced pertains to *forgiveness*. If, as the case makes clear, the wrongdoer is "fallen" and is gripped by some self-diminishing power, then there is a sense in which the wrongdoer may be *excused* for doing what she did. But then, the wisdom evinced is the propensity to excuse when excuse is called for. As I argued in Part I, forgiveness is directed at *responsible wrongdoing*.[54] Otherwise, forgiveness would lack an arena of its own, and this is true regardless of how prone we are to confuse forgiveness with excuse. Thus, as Murphy puts it, "Father forgive them for they know not what they do" goes better as "Father *excuse* them for they know not what they do."[55]

Finally, I would be remiss if I did not make mention of yet another reason we sometimes consider in tendering forgiveness—namely, that we ourselves are in need of forgiveness. This, presumably, is the point of the parable of the unforgiving servant in the gospel of Matthew.[56] Since during the course of our lives we engage in behavior that is injurious to ourselves, we ourselves are in need of forgiveness. Because of this, we ought to forgive those who have injured us. Construed in this manner, forgiveness has roots in the virtue of *humility*.[57]

From my point of view, it is of course true that to err is human and that we all sometimes fail in fulfilling the requirements of moral decency. However, I do not think this is a good reason to forgive, if only because, in the forgiveness situation, our own moral history is not at issue. Therefore, regardless of whether we ourselves stand in need of forgiveness, such a reason cannot be countenanced.

Closing Comments

In the final analysis, I have identified just one good reason we may use to forgive—and that is because the wrongdoer has repented. I have endeavored to show that, if forgiveness is to be valued as a moral response, it must be for a reason that permits the lifting of the victim's resentment. In the absence of repentance, forgiveness betrays a lack of self-respect. It also collapses into condonation of wrongdoing, and it is wrong to condone wrongful behavior.

However we go about deciding when to tender forgiveness, there is no denying that the forgiving of wrongdoers is risky business. Inevitably, it entails placing trust in another's good-will when such trust has previously been violated. Certainly, to forgive a wrongdoer for a wrong she has done is to leave oneself open to further misconduct. Descartes once said, "It is prudent never to trust wholly those things which have once deceived us."[58] And this applies as much to people as it does to the senses. When the wrongdoer forgiven is a repeat offender, the risk incurred is doubly great.

Notwithstanding, as Sissela Bok has pointed out, trust is the atmosphere in which what matters to us thrives,[59] and one of the things that matters to us is harmonious relations with our fellow human beings. However, harmonious relations is not all that matters to us; we are also concerned with our own self-respect. This is why forgiveness of wrongdoers in the absence of repentance is morally troublesome. I might also add that it is bad policy, since it leaves us vulnerable to further misconduct. While a wrongdoer's repentance hardly insures us against future injury, if we are to tender forgiveness to anyone at all, we must risk our trust, while hoping that repentance will mitigate this risk. Perhaps, when all is said and done, this is why forgiveness is often applauded. For in forgiving a wrongdoer, we tacitly affirm the importance of trust alongside such notions as self-respect.

Notes

Introduction

1. P. F. Strawson, "Freedom and Resentment," *Proceedings of the British Academy*, 48 (1962), reprinted in Strawson's *Freedom and Resentment and Other Essays* (Oxford, England: Methuen, 1974), p. 6.

2. See R. S. Downie, "Forgiveness," *Philosophical Quarterly*, 15 (April 1965), pp. 128–34.

3. See Jeffrie G. Murphy, "Forgiveness and Resentment," *Midwest Studies in Philosophy*, 7 (1982), pp. 503–16.

4. See Elizabeth Beardsley, "Understanding and Forgiveness," in *The Philosophy of Brand Blanshard*, ed. Paul A. Schlipp (LaSalle, Ill.: Open Court, 1980), pp. 247–58.

5. See Martin Golding, "Forgiveness and Regret," *Philosophical Forum*, 16, nos. 1–2 (Fall/Winter 1984–1985), pp. 121–37.

6. See G. E. M. Anscombe, "Modern Moral Philosophy," *Philosophy*, 33 (1958), pp. 1–19.

7. See Alasdair MacIntyre, *After Virtue*, 2nd ed. (Notre Dame, Ind.: University of Notre Dame Press, 1984).

8. See William Frankena, *Ethics*, 2nd ed. (Englewood Cliffs, N.J.: Prentice-Hall, 1973), chap. 4.

9. See Murphy, "Forgiveness and Resentment," pp. 504–5.

10. John Stuart Mill, "Remarks on Bentham's Philosophy," in *Collected Works*, vol. 10, ed. J. M. Robson (Toronto, Canada: University of Toronto Press, 1968), pp. 7–8.

11. Strawson, "Freedom and Resentment," p. 5.

12. For a discussion of Feuerbach and others on this matter, see Allan Wood, *Kant's Moral Religion* (Ithaca, N.Y.: Cornell University Press, 1970), chap. 6.

13. See Joseph Butler, *Fifteen Sermons* (London: The English Theological Library, 1726), sermon 8 ("Upon Resentment") and sermon 9 ("Upon Forgiveness of Injuries").

14. See generally, Friedrich Nietzsche, *Beyond Good and Evil*, trans. Walter

Kaufmann (New York: Vintage Books, 1966); see also Nietzsche, *On the Genealogy of Morals and Ecce Homo*, trans. Walter Kaufmann (New York: Vintage Books, 1969).

15. See Plutarch, "On the Control of Anger," in *Moralia*, vol. 6 (London: Heinemann, 1958).

16. See Lucius Seneca, "On Anger," in *Moral Essays*, vol. 1 (Cambridge, Mass.: Harvard University Press, 1958).

17. Hannah Arendt, "Irreversibility and the Power to Forgive," in *The Human Condition* (Chicago: University of Chicago Press, 1958), p. 238.

18. Aurel Kolnai, "Forgiveness," in *Ethics, Value and Reality: Selected Papers of Aurel Kolnai*, eds. Bernard Williams and David Wiggins (Indianapolis, Ind.: Hackett, 1978), p. 211.

19. William Neblett, "Forgiveness and Ideals," *Mind*, 83 (April 1974), p. 275.

20. R. J. O'Shaughnessy, "Forgiveness," *Philosophy*, 42 (October 1967), p. 351.

21. Joanna North, "Wrongdoing and Forgiveness," *Philosophy*, 62, no. 242 (October 1987), p. 499.

22. Uma Narayan, "Varieties of Forgiveness," an unpublished paper presented at the American Philosophical Association, Eastern Division, 86th Annual Meeting, Atlanta, 1989.

23. Neblett, "Forgiveness and Ideals," p. 269.

24. Ibid., p. 272.

25. Murphy, "Forgiveness and Resentment," pp. 507–8.

26. See Philippa Foot, "Virtues and Vices," in *Virtues and Vices and Other Essays in Moral Philosophy* (Berkeley: University of California Press, 1978), chap. 1.

27. See Peter Geach, *The Virtues* (Cambridge, England: Cambridge University Press, 1977). Geach says, "Endurance or defiance of danger in pursuance of a wrong end is not virtuous and in my book is not courageous either" (p. 160).

28. See George Henrik von Wright, *The Varieties of Goodness* (London: Routledge & Kegan Paul, 1963), chap. 7.

29. This is the position put forward by Foot, whose reasoning I find compelling. According to Foot, virtue words (e.g., "courage") are analogous to such words as "solvent" and "poison" in that they are powers for producing actions and desires. Notwithstanding, just as solvents and poisons sometimes fail to act in characteristic ways, so it is with the virtues. "Just as we might say in a certain setting, 'P is not a poison here,' though P is a poison and P is here, so we might say that industriousness, or temperance, is not a virtue in some." "Virtues and Vices," p. 17.

Gregory Pence, for one, is unconvinced by this argument. "If one argues by analogy, one lives or dies by the tightness of 'fit' and to say courage 'operates' in the hero but not in the murderer is like saying batteries 'operate' when they start cars but not when they power electroshock machines." "Recent Work on the Virtues," *American Philosophical Quarterly*, 21, no. 4 (October 1984), p. 288. This rebuttal, however, is unsatisfactory. Whether a battery is used to start cars or whether it is used to power electroshock machines, the battery is used *as a battery*. Suppose, however, that a battery is used to hold down paper. Then, though B is a battery and B is here, it does not follow that B is a battery here. By analogous reasoning, though courage is a virtue and courage is here, it does not follow that courage is a virtue here. Thus—Pence to the contrary—Foot's position is not without merit.

It is, however, the minority position. In addition to von Wright and Pence, James Wallace has argued, "One can act from motives that are morally reprehensible and still show courage." He cites favorably from Protagoras, who claimed that a man can be brave but possess no other virtue. James Wallace, *Virtues and Vices* (Ithaca, N.Y.: Cornell University Press, 1978), p. 77. As I see it, however, if what we mean by virtue is a fixed disposition, habit, or trait to do what is morally commendable, then we cannot show virtue in pursuing evil ends. We can show a trait that would otherwise be a virtue if directed toward good ends (i.e., we could show courage, temperance, honesty, etc.), but it would not count as virtue if directed toward evil. Because of this, I would count the "virtues" as virtues of form only. They do not become *moral* virtues unless guided by moral principles. See Derek L. Phillips, "Authenticiteit or Moraliteit?" *Wijsgerig Perspectief op Maatschappij en Wetenschap*, 22 (1982), reprinted as "Authenticity or Morality?" in *The Virtues; Contemporary Essays on Moral Character*, eds. Robert Kruschwitz and Robert C. Roberts (Belmont, Calif.: Wadsworth Publishing, 1987), pp. 23–35. I might also add that, were virtue to be displayed in morally bad actions, it would be hard to make sense of such intelligible phrases as "being honest to a fault."

30. Murphy, "Forgiveness and Resentment," p. 508.

31. We can, for instance, forgive for a *cause*. See Anne Minas, "God and Forgiveness," *Philosophical Quarterly*, 25 (April 1975), p. 144.

32. See Minas, "God and Forgiveness," pp. 138–50. For a philosophical analysis of a theological model, see Marilyn Adams, "Forgiveness: A Christian Model," *Faith and Philosophy*, 8, no. 3 (July 1991). I thank William Alston for bringing this to my attention.

33. Minas, "God and Forgiveness," pp. 138–50.

34. See Meirlys Lewis, "On Forgiveness," *Philosophical Quarterly*, 30 (July 1980), pp. 236–45.

35. John Gingell, "Forgiveness and Power," *Analysis*, 34, no. 6 (June 1974), pp. 180–83.

36. Ibid., p. 182.

37. See Fyodor Dostoyevsky, "Rebellion," in *The Brothers Karamazov*, trans. Constance Garnett (New York: Signet Classics, 1980), pp. 223–26.

38. See Herbert Morris, "Murphy on Forgiveness," *Criminal Justice Ethics*, 7, no. 2 (1988), pp. 15–19.

39. Ibid., pp. 17.
40. Ibid.
41. Ibid.
42. For his doctrine of analogy, see Aquinas, *Summa de Veritate Catholicae Didei contra Gentiles* (1259–1264), bk. I, chs. 28–34, reprinted as *St. Thomas Aquinas: On the Truth of the Catholic Faith*, trans. A. C. Pegis, et al. (New York: Doubleday, 1955).

1 What Forgiveness Is Not

1. For more on the concept of injury, see Chapter 2. Jean Hampton observes that an injury occurs when we fail to give people the treatment they deserve. However, "this 'objective' injury (an injury based upon what one takes the correct moral or societal facts about self-worth to be) is usually—although it need not be—associated with a subjective injury." "Forgiveness, Resentment, and Hatred," in *Forgiveness and Mercy*, Jeffrie G. Murphy and Jean Hampton (New York: Cambridge University Press, 1988), p. 45.
2. Anthony Flew, "The Justification of Punishment," *Philosophy*, 29 (October 1954), p. 291.
3. See Hampton, "Forgiveness, Resentment, and Hatred," pp. 37–38.
4. Thus, though we will have occasion to speak of the locution "I forgive you," we should be understood to mean "I forgive you for ———," and what follows the "for ———" is as much a part of forgiveness as "I forgive you." Logically put, "forgiveness" is a three-place predicate represented symbolically as Fabc. "F" is the predicate letter for "forgiveness," "a" and "b" range over people, and "c" ranges over wrongful actions.
5. P. F. Strawson, "Freedom and Resentment," *Proceedings of the British Academy*, 48 (1962), reprinted in *Freedom and Resentment and Other Essays*, ed. P. F. Strawson (Oxford, England: Methuen, 1974), p. 6.
6. Since I later argue that one ought not to forgive a wrongdoer in the absence of repentance, the question might be raised whether forgiving the dead is ever a virtue. As I see it, forgiving the dead can count as a virtue if there is evidence to believe that the deceased person *would have* repented, had time permitted.
7. Anne Minas, "God and Forgiveness," *Philosophical Quarterly*, 25, no. 99 (April 1975), pp. 138–39.
8. While Minas uses this example, it is not at all clear how one can judge murder to be anything but wrong since, to paraphrase Descartes, the will ordinarily follows the understanding in such cases. One may believe that what was done was not murder, but that is a different matter. Also different are cases where the rightness or wrongness of an action is a question on which there is reasonable disagreement.
9. Hampton, "Forgiveness, Resentment, and Hatred," pp. 84–85.

10. For an excellent discussion on the differences between an ethics of "being" and an ethics of "doing," see Bernard Mayo, *Ethics and the Moral Life* (London: Macmillan, 1958), pp. 211–14.

11. This argument is discussed in Robert B. Louden, "On Some Vices of Virtue Ethics," *American Philosophical Quarterly*, 21 (July 1984), pp. 227–36.

12. Hampton, "Forgiveness, Resentment, and Hatred," p. 86.

13. Ibid, p. 84.

14. It is not at all clear that it is possible, let alone sensible, to *try* to have the change of heart Hampton suggests. Bernard Williams has referred to such efforts as "willing to believe" and has argued that it is self-defeating. See Bernard Williams, "Deciding to Believe," in *Problems of the Self* (Cambridge, England: Cambridge University Press, 1973).

15. See Thomas Hobbes, *Leviathan* (1651), ed. C. B. Macpherson (Harmondsworth, England, and New York: Penguin Books, 1979), pp. 533–36 (pt. 3, chap. 42).

16. Minas, "God and Forgiveness," p. 140.

17. Alwynne Smart makes what is essentially the same point in connection with mercy. See "Mercy," *Philosophy*, 43 (October 1968), pp. 345–59. Smart argues that the remission or modification of punishment in the light of special circumstances surrounding a crime is not a true case of mercy, but only a case of making a judgment about the appropriate punishment, taking all relevant considerations into account.

18. See R. J. O'Shaughnessy, "Forgiveness," *Philosophy*, 42 (October 1967), pp. 336–51.

19. Ibid., p. 337.

20. Ibid.

21. Ibid., p. 338.

22. Ibid.

23. Ibid.

24. See Joseph Butler, *Fifteen Sermons* (London: The English Theological Library, 1726), sermon 7 ("Upon Resentment") and sermon 9 ("Upon Forgiveness of Injuries").

25. See Arthur Danto, *Nietzsche as Philosopher* (New York: Macmillan, 1965). Max Scheler once explained Nietzsche's insight thus: "Revenge . . . , based as it is upon an experience of impotence, is always primarily a matter of those who are 'weak' in some respect." Max Scheler, *Ressentiment*, trans. Holdheim (New York: Free Press, 1961), p. 46.

26. See Butler, sermon 8 ("Upon Resentment").

27. Kathleen Dean Moore, *Pardons: Justice, Mercy, and the Public Interest* (New York: Oxford University Press, 1989), p. 184.

28. A. C. Ewing, *The Morality of Punishment* (Montclair, N.J.: Patterson-Smith, 1970), p. 31.

29. Martin Hughes, "Forgiveness," *Analysis*, 35, no. 4 (March 1975), p. 113.

30. R. S. Downie, "Forgiveness," *Philosophical Quarterly*, 15 (April 1965), p. 134.
31. Jeffrie G. Murphy, "Forgiveness and Resentment," *Midwest Studies in Philosophy*, 7 (1982), p. 508.
32. Ibid. There is, however, an important difference between overcoming resentment and forgetting. The former engages the will in a way that the latter does not. Thus, it is not at all clear that forgiveness is as easily confused with forgetting as Murphy suggests. I owe this observation to Walter Brand.
33. Murphy, "Forgiveness and Resentment," p. 508.
34. See H. J. N. Horsbrugh, "Forgiveness," *Canadian Journal of Philosophy*, 4, no. 2 (December 1974), pp. 273–74.
35. Ibid., p. 273.
36. Ibid., p. 271.
37. Ibid., p. 270.
38. Murphy, "Forgiveness and Resentment," p. 504.
39. See Martin Golding, "Forgiveness and Regret," *Philosophical Forum*, 16, nos. 1–2 (Fall/Winter 1984–1985).
40. Horsbrugh, "Forgiveness," p. 279.
41. Ibid., pp. 278–79.
42. This is reminiscent of Isaiah Berlin's strictures against confounding what one wants with what one *really* wants. See "Two Concepts of Liberty," in *Four Essays on Liberty* (New York: Oxford University Press, 1979), p. 133.
43. See Kurt Baier, "The Meaning of Life," in *Philosophy: The Basic Issues*, 2nd ed., eds. E. D. Klemke, David Kline, and Robert Hollinger (New York: St. Martin's Press, 1986), p. 357.
44. See the last section of Chapter 2. As I shall argue, the overcoming of resentment (or the commitment to try to overcome it) is a necessary condition only for the paradigmatic use of the expression "I forgive you."
45. At least it is impossible for the *wrongdoer* to know whether his victim has forgiven him or simply forgotten the relevant incident. But I also suspect that the victim himself may be unable to distinguish between forgiving and forgetting after there has elapsed a great deal of time.
46. It can be argued that the asymmetry discussed here is psychologically—rather than logically—disturbing.
47. Hampton, "Forgiveness, Resentment, and Hatred," p. 36.
48. Ibid., p. 43n.
49. Moore, *Pardons*, p. 185.
50. See Norvin Richards, "Forgiveness," *Ethics*, 99, no. 1 (October 1988), pp. 77–79.
51. See the "Resentment" section in Chapter 2.
52. See Joseph Beatty, "Forgiveness," *American Philosophical Quarterly*, 7, no. 3 (July 1970), pp. 246–52.
53. Ibid., p. 246.
54. Ibid., pp. 249–51.

55. Ibid.

56. See William Neblett, "Forgiveness and Ideals," *Mind*, 83 (April 1974), pp. 269–75.

57. See O'Shaughnessy, "Forgiveness."

58. This point was made by Michael Dummett in "Truth," *Proceedings of the Aristotelian Society*, 59 (1958–1959), pp. 141–62, reprinted in *Philosophical Logic*, ed. P. F. Strawson (London: Oxford University Press, 1967), esp. pp. 51 and 68.

59. See O'Shaughnessy, p. 344.

60. Shakespeare, *The Tempest*, act 5, scene 1, cited in O'Shaughnessy, "Forgiveness," p. 340.

61. O'Shaughnessy, "Forgiveness," p. 341.

62. As quoted in ibid., p. 346.

63. Ibid.

64. Neblett, "Forgiveness and Ideals," p. 275.

65. Dummett, "Truth."

66. See Aurel Kolnai, "Forgiveness," in *Ethics, Value, and Reality: Selected Papers of Aurel Kolnai*, eds. Bernard Williams and David Wiggins (Indianapolis, Ind.: Hackett, 1978), p. 222.

2 What Forgiveness Is

1. See J. L. Austin, *How to Do Things with Words* (Cambridge, Mass.: Harvard University Press, 1962). My analysis of forgiveness owes much to Elizabeth Beardsley. See Elizabeth Beardsley, "Understanding and Forgiveness," in *The Philosophy of Brand Blanshard*, ed. Paul Schlipp (LaSalle, Ill.: Open Court, 1980), pp. 247–57.

2. Austin, *How to Do*, pp. 159–60.

3. Ibid. p. 159.

4. Ibid.

5. Ibid., p. 151.

6. Ibid., p. 159.

7. For a useful discussion of the notion of behabitives, see Elizabeth Beardsley, "Moral Disapproval and Moral Indignation," *Philosophy and Phenomenological Research*, 31 (1970), p. 163.

8. For a similar analysis of "blame," see ibid. To a great extent, I have applied Beardsley's analysis of "blame" to an analysis of "forgiveness."

9. Austin, *How to Do*, p. 159.

10. I owe this example to William Neblett, "Forgiveness and Ideals," *Mind*, 83 (April 1974), p. 275.

11. The objection may be raised that not all expressions of attitudes are performative utterances, and so of any one utterance we are not sure if *it* functions as a performative. Austin, for instance, mentions "don't mind" as

an exmple of a behabitive that expresses an attitude. *How to Do*, p. 159. And while "don't mind" may be a report of how one feels rather than the expression of how one feels, the relevant point is that it can function as either. Austin himself admits, "There are obvious connexions with both stating or describing what our feelings are and expressing in the sense of venting our feelings, though behabitives are distinct from both of these." Ibid.

12. For an argument to this effect, see William P. Alston, "Moral Attitudes and Moral Judgments," *Nous*, 2 (1968), pp. 1–23.

13. I have borrowed this terminology from Beardsley, "Understanding and Forgiveness," p. 249.

14. H. J. N. Horsbrugh, "Forgiveness," *Canadian Journal of Philosophy*, 4, no. 2 (December 1974), p. 279.

15. There are no less than four points that need to be made here. First, in speaking of moral wrongdoing, I intend to be neutral with respect to consequentialism and deontologism. Second, I speak of moral wrongdoing only within the framework of the Judeo-Christian tradition. Third, my conception of moral wrongdoing includes both acts of commission as well as "acts" of omission. Fourth and finally, though I discuss forgiveness primarily in the context of rights violation, there is a sense in which one can do wrong without violating a particular right. One can, for instance, wrong someone by failing to remember that person's birthday. Uma Narayan, for instance, maintains that we wrong other people when we fail to live up to what she calls "reasonable expectations." "Varieties of Forgiveness," unpublished paper delivered at the American Philosophical Association, Eastern Division, 86th Annual Meeting, Atlanta, 1989.

However, I am primarily concerned with the ordinary interpersonal situation where one individual wrongs another by infringing on that person's rights.

16. See Jeffrie G. Murphy, "Forgiveness and Resentment," *Midwest Studies in Philosophy*, 7 (1982), p. 506. See also Beardsley, "Understanding and Forgiveness," p. 250; and Aurel Kolnai, "Forgiveness," in *Ethics, Value, and Reality: Selected Papers of Aurel Kolnai*, eds. Bernard Williams and David Wiggins (Indianapolis, Ind.: Hackett Publishing, 1978), p. 215. Needless to say, I do not wish to disallow this sort of behavior; I merely refuse to include it as a part of the paradigm.

17. J. L. Austin, "A Plea for Excuses," *Proceedings of the Aristotelian Society*, 57 (1956–1957), pp. 1–30, reprinted in *The Philosophy of Action*, ed. Alan White (Oxford, England: Oxford University Press, 1968), p. 20. For a rather different and less eccentric definition of "justification," see Virginia Held, *Rights and Goods: Justifying Social Action* (New York: Free Press, 1984), pp. 31–33. See also Tom Beauchamp, "The Justification of Moral Beliefs," in *Philosophical Ethics: An Introduction to Moral Philosophy*, ed. Tom Beauchamp (New York: McGraw-Hill, 1982), pp. 303–9.

18. Austin, "A Plea for Excuses," p. 20.

19. See Anthony Kenny, *Wittgenstein* (Cambridge, Mass.: Harvard University Press, 1974), p. 224.

20. Horsbrugh, for one, refers to what I call the paradigm case as the "standard case" of forgiveness. See "Forgiveness," p. 271.

21. See the section "Austin's Second Condition and Third-party Forgiveness."

22. P. F. Strawson, "Freedom and Resentment," *Proceedings of the British Academy*, 48 (1962), reprinted in *Freedom and Resentment and Other Essays*, ed. P. F. Strawson (Oxford, England: Methuen, 1974), pp. 6–7. As Rousseau said (somewhere), "the nature of things does not madden us; only ill-will does."

23. See W. D. Ross, *The Right and the Good* (1930) (Indianapolis, Ind.: Hackett Publishing, 1988), pp. 18–36. I agree with both Strawson and Ross that the expression of ill-will (or lack of good-will) is a necessary feature of moral injury. Thus, in my view, Jones may injure Smith by failing to remember Smith's birthday; but the injury that occurs is not a moral one, owing to Jones's forgetfulness. This being so, I refuse to allow this sort of injury to be an appropriate subject for forgiving behavior. Rather, it would be an appropriate subject for Smith's *excusing* Jones. Of course, Smith may *say* he forgives Jones, and Jones may understand the way in which Smith uses the term; but if forgiveness is to have an arena of its own, such distinctions need to be drawn. Needless to say, I do not deny that forgiveness and excuse share many similarities. See note 100 below.

24. See R. B. Brandt, "A Moral Principle about Killing," in *Intervention and Reflection: Basic Issues in Medical Ethics*, 2nd ed., ed. Ronald Munson (Belmont, Calif.: Wadsworth Publishing, 1983), p. 175. In this article Brandt is concerned with showing that mercy killings are noninjurious killings.

25. For a discussion of the ethics of resentment, see Chapter 4.

26. This is the way the term has been employed by those who have written on resentment. See Murphy, "Forgiveness and Resentment," p. 507. See also Andrew von Hirsch and Nils Jareborg, "Provocation and Culpability," in *Responsibility, Character, and the Emotions: New Essays in Moral Psychology*, ed. Ferdinand Schoeman (New York: Cambridge University Press, 1987), pp. 248–49.

27. See Joel Feinberg, "Justice and Personal Desert," in *Doing and Deserving: Essays in the Theory of Responsibility*, ed. Joel Feinberg (Princeton, N.J.: Princeton University Press, 1970), pp. 70–71.

28. Pascal, *Pensées* (1662), trans. A. J. Krailsheimer (New York: Penguin Classics, 1984), no. 412. The complete quotation is as follows: "Man's war within [is] between his Reason and his Passions. . . . As Man has both, he cannot be free from war, since he cannot be at peace with the one without being at war with the other. So he is always divided, and always his own adversary."

29. See Robert Solomon, *The Passions* (Garden City, N.Y.: Anchor Press, 1976), pp. 1–23. (It is Solomon who refers to this view as the "received view.")

30. See Bernard Williams, "Morality and the Emotions," in *Problems of the Self* (Cambridge, England: Cambridge University Press, 1973).

31. See William Lyons, *Emotions* (Cambridge, England: Cambridge University Press, 1980).

32. See Strawson, "Freedom and Resentment," esp. pp. 6–8.

33. Joseph Butler, *Fifteen Sermons* (London: The English Theological Library, 1726), sermon 8 ("Upon Resentment"), p. 121.

34. Ibid., pp. 117–18.

35. Strawson, "Freedom and Resentment," p. 7.

36. Jean Hampton, "Forgiveness, Resentment, and Hatred," in *Forgiveness and Mercy*, Jeffrie G. Murphy and Jean Hampton (New York: Cambridge University Press, 1988), pp. 54–55.

37. Von Hirsch and Jareborg, "Provocation and Culpability," p. 248.

38. Feinberg, "Justice and Desert," p. 70.

39. Murphy, "Forgiveness and Resentment," p. 507.

40. Feinberg, "Justice and Desert," p. 71.

41. More precisely: "Punishment is punishment only where it is deserved." F. H. Bradley, *Ethical Studies*, 2nd ed. (Oxford, England: Oxford University Press, 1927), pp. 26–27.

42. Ibid., p. 68; emphasis added.

43. Von Hirsch and Jareborg, "Provocation and Culpability," p. 248; emphasis added.

44. For an analysis of third-party forgiveness, see the section "Austin's Second Condition and Third-party Forgiveness," in Chapter 2.

45. See Murphy, "Forgiveness and Resentment," p. 505; and Martin Golding, "Forgiveness and Regret," *Philosophical Forum*, 16, nos. 1–2 (Fall/Winter 1984–1985), p. 131.

46. For a competing view of blame, see Beardsley, "Moral Disapproval and Moral Indignation," pp. 165–66.

47. This is reminiscent of "Mill's Howler." According to some interpretations, Mill thought "desirable" meant "is desired" rather than "ought to be desired." In an analogous way, it would be a howler to think that "blamable" meant "is blamed" rather than "ought to be blamed."

48. Joel Feinberg, "Action and Responsibility," in *Doing and Deserving*, p. 127. Elizabeth Beardsley writes, "An agent X is blameworthy to some degree for his act A if and only if:

1) Act A is a breach of a moral rule;
2) Act A was performed voluntarily;
3) Agent X, in performing A, was not acting in ignorance of relevant facts; and
4) The desire felt by X which was dominant in causing him to commit act A was in that situation a bad desire."

See Elizabeth Beardsley, "Moral Worth and Moral Credit," *Philosophical Review*, 66 (1957), pp. 3, 4, and 28, reprinted in *Moral Philosophy: Contemporary Texts and Contemporary Problems*, eds. Joel Feinberg and Henry West (Encino, Calif.: Dickerson Publishing, 1977), p. 472.

49. L. C. Holborow, "Praise, Blame, and Credit," *Proceedings of the Aristotelian Society*, 72 (1971–1972).

50. Murphy, "Forgiveness and Resentment," p. 508.

51. See Thomas E. Hill, Jr., "Servility and Self-respect," *Monist*, 62 (January 1969), pp. 87–88.

52. See Hampton, "Forgiveness, Resentment, and Hatred," pp. 43–54.

53. For a good discussion of Nietzsche's views on this subject, see Michael S. Moore, "The Moral Worth of Retribution," in *Responsibility, Character, and the Emotions*, pp. 191–217.

54. Jeffrie Murphy brought this to my attention.

55. P. Twambley, "Mercy and Forgiveness," *Analysis*, 36 (January 1976), p. 89.

56. See Norvin Richards, "Forgiveness," *Ethics*, 99, no. 1 (October 1988), pp. 77–97.

57. Ibid., pp. 77–79.

58. J. L. Austin, "Performative-Constative," in *The Philosophy of Language*, ed. J. R. Searle (Oxford, England: Oxford University Press, 1977), p. 13.

59. Austin, *How to Do*, pp. 13–14.

60. See William Alston's *Philosophy of Language* (Englewood Cliffs, N.J.: Prentice-Hall, 1964), chap. 2.

61. Austin, *How to Do*, p. 16.

62. Austin uses these terms to criticize *actions* as opposed to statements.

63. Austin, *How to Do*, p. 16.

64. See p. 48 of ibid. for a discussion of Moore's sense of "implies."

65. This is Austin's example. See J. L. Austin, "Performative Utterances," in *Philosophical Papers* (New York: Oxford University Press, 1970), p. 237.

66. While Austin does not explicitly include "I forgive you" on his list of performatives, he does hint that it is to be included. See p. 45 of *How to Do*.

67. Ibid., p. 27.

68. Ibid., p. 24. Austin's example is reminiscent of the comical scene from *Man of La Mancha* in which Don Quixote is "knighted" Knight of the Woeful Countenance by a drunkard following a bar brawl in which Quixote comes to the rescue of his beloved Dulcinea.

69. See Fyodor Dostoyevsky, *The Brothers Karamazov* (1880), trans. Constance Garnett (New York: Signet Classics, 1957), pp. 223–26.

70. Ibid. It is not entirely clear whether Ivan Karamazov is arguing that the boy's mother cannot or ought not to forgive the general. As Alyosha understands Ivan, it is both. Thus, Alyosha says, "But, Ivan, you asked just now, is there a person in the whole world who has the right to forgive and can forgive?" (p. 226). As I see it, both of these questions are being addressed by Ivan, though I am using this passage from the novel to illustrate the logic as opposed to the ethics of forgiveness.

71. Simon Wiesenthal, *The Sunflower* (London: W. H. Allen, 1972), p. 57.

72. Ibid., p. 119.
73. Ibid., p. 131.
74. Ibid., p. 173.
75. Horsbrugh, "Forgiveness," p. 274.
76. See John Stuart Mill, *Utilitarianism* (1863) (Indianapolis, Ind.: Hackett Publishing, 1979), p. 34: "The only proof capable of being given that an object is visible is that people actually see it. The only proof that a sound is audible is that people hear it. . . . In like manner, I apprehend, the sole evidence it is possible to produce that anything is desirable is that people do actually desire it." Of course, it has often been pointed out that "desirable" has a logic that is different from "visible" and "audible."
77. See note 47 above and accompanying text.
78. See Horsbrugh, "Forgiveness," p. 274.
79. Douglas V. Steere, ed., *Spiritual Counsels and Letters of Baron von Hugel* (London: Darton, Longman, and Todd, 1959), p. 22.
80. Horsbrugh, "Forgiveness," p. 275.
81. Ibid.
82. Ibid., pp. 275–76. Against Horsbrugh's analysis, one may argue that the standing needed to forgive is not the same standing that is needed to desist from forgiving.
83. William Neblett, "Forgiveness and Ideals," *Mind*, 83 (April 1974), p. 271.
84. See the section "Resentment" earlier in this chapter.
85. Jeffrie Murphy was of help in developing such an argument.
86. Strawson, "Freedom and Resentment," p. 14.
87. Ibid.
88. Hampton, "Forgiveness, Resentment, and Hatred," p. 59.
89. The reference to Prince Myshkin is especially significant, as it has often been pointed out that Myshkin is Christ-like, suggesting the question of whether priests (i.e., third parties) can forgive, as they are empowered to do in the Catholic religion. Assuming that priests—by virtue of their calling—are uniquely concerned with the suffering of all Catholics, I see no problem with their granting third-party forgiveness. Of course, whether their calling enables them to do so as an empirical matter is another question. There is an enormous variation in the degree to which people can psychologically identify with the sufferings of others.

It should also be pointed out that third-party forgiveness is unique to Catholicism. In Judaism, a well-known Rabbinical dictum says that, while Yom Kippur atones for sins between man and God, it does not atone for sins committed between man and his neighbor. See M. Yoma 8:5.

90. Austin, *How to Do*, p. 37.
91. Austin, "Performative-Constative," p. 14.
92. Ibid., pp. 14–15.
93. See Alston, "Moral Attitudes and Judgments," pp. 1–23.

94. See J. O. Urmson, "John Langshaw Austin," in the *Encyclopedia of Philosophy* (New York: Macmillan Publishing, 1967).

95. See R. J. O'Shaughnessy, "Forgiveness," *Philosophy*, 42 (October 1967), pp. 336–51. See also Chapter 1.

96. Austin frequently refers to the "force" of performatives. See, for example, *How to Do*, p. 147.

97. Ibid, p. 159.

98. For a general account of the virtues of this type of analysis, see J. R. Searle, "Introduction," in *The Philosophy of Language*, pp. 1–12. I have, throughout this essay, ignored many problems concerning Austin's doctrine, such as the relationship between thinking and speaking, and so forth.

99. Ibid., p. 7.

100. More precisely, what I have sought to put forward is an explication of forgiveness designed to clarify our familiar but imprecise use of the term. My account, in some ways, resembles a lexical definition, inasmuch as it partially describes what is thought to be correct usage of the term. Yet, my account also proposes a new or amended use. That is, it transforms an old imprecise use into a more exact, more clearly delineated, one. Consequently, in evaluating my analysis, it would be a mistake to judge it as if it were nothing but a stipulative definition. The analysis as a whole must be judged on its merits as a proposal.

101. Kathleen Dean Moore, *Pardons: Justice, Mercy, and the Public Interest* (New York: Oxford University Press, 1989), p. 105.

102. Horsbrugh, "Forgiveness," p. 270.

103. Austin, *How to Do*, pp. 150–63.

104. Needless to say, I am speaking here and in the preceding examples of *sincerely* uttering the words in question. It is, of course, quite easy to utter the words in question if what we mean by "utter" is the vocal production of the relevant sounds. It is not, however, easy to utter the relevant sounds sincerely and meaningfully. The pop singer Tracy Chapman has said this in one of her songs: "Forgive me. These words are hard to say."

105. R. S. Downie, "Forgiveness," *Philosophical Quarterly*, 15 (April 1965), p. 131.

3 Other Things Forgiveness Is Not

1. I mean condonation in its nonlegal sense. Black's Law Dictionary defines "condonation" as "the conditional remission of forgiveness, by means of continuance of resumption of marital cohabitation."

2. See Aurel Kolnai, "Forgiveness," in *Ethics, Value, and Reality: Selected Papers of Aurel Kolnai*, eds. Bernard Williams and David Wiggins (Indianapolis, Ind.: Hackett Publishing, 1978), pp. 215–16. See also Jean Hampton, "Forgiveness, Resentment, and Hatred," in *Forgiveness and*

Mercy, Jeffrie Murphy and Jean Hampton (New York: Cambridge University Press, 1988), pp. 39–41.

3. Hampton, "Forgiveness, Resentment, and Hatred," p. 40.

4. Kolnai, "Forgiveness," p. 215.

5. Ibid.

6. Sir Edward Coke, *The Third Part of the Institutes of the Laws of England*, 1817, p. 233.

7. Herbert Morris, "Persons and Punishment," *Monist*, 52, no. 4 (October 1968), p. 478.

8. Jeffrie G. Murphy, "Forgiveness and Resentment," *Midwest Studies in Philosophy*, 7 (1982), p. 509.

9. See Susan Jacoby, *Wild Justice: The Evolution of Revenge* (New York: Harper & Row, 1983), p. 349.

10. Kathleen Dean Moore, *Pardons: Justice, Mercy, and the Public Interest* (New York: Oxford University Press, 1989), p. 193.

11. R. S. Downie, "Forgiveness," *Philosophical Quarterly*, 15 (April 1965), p. 131.

12. Ibid., p. 132.

13. See Chapter 1, the section "Forgiveness as the Remission of Punishment."

14. Or moral order *alone*.

15. See Downie, "Forgiveness," pp. 132–33.

16. See J. L. Austin, *How to Do Things with Words* (Cambridge, Mass.: Harvard University Press, 1962), pp. 154–55.

17. Ibid., p. 154.

18. Ibid., pp. 154–55.

19. Ibid., p. 156.

20. Downie, "Forgiveness," p. 132.

21. See Moore, *Pardons*, p. 193.

22. See Henry Sidgwick, *The Methods of Ethics* (1874), 7th ed. (London: Macmillan, 1963), bk. 3, chap. 5.

23. *Burdick v. United States*, 236 U.S. 90 (1915).

24. Moore, *Pardons*, p. 195.

25. Alwynne Smart, "Mercy," *Philosophy*, 43 (October 1968), pp. 345–59, reprinted in *The Philosophy of Punishment*, ed. B. B. Acton (New York: St. Martin's Press, 1969), pp. 212–27.

26. Ibid., p. 345.

27. Ibid., p. 350.

28. Ibid., pp. 358–59.

29. See Claudia Card, "Mercy," *Philosophical Review* (April 1972), pp. 182–207.

30. Ibid.

31. See P. Twambley, "Mercy and Forgiveness," *Analysis*, 36 (January 1976), p. 84–90.

32. Ibid., p. 85.
33. Ibid.
34. Ibid., pp. 85–86.
35. Ibid., p. 86.
36. See Jeffrie G. Murphy, "Mercy and Legal Justice," in *Forgiveness and Mercy*, pp. 174–76.
37. Ibid., p. 175.
38. More precisely, mercy consists in refusing to press a right, rather than in waiving a right.
39. While Murphy subscribes to this view in "Mercy and Legal Justice," p. 166, it is not at all clear that Twambley in "Mercy and Forgiveness" does as well.

4 The Ethics of Resentment

1. Goldie Bristle and Carol McGinnis, *When It's Hard to Forgive* (Wheaton, Ill.: Victor Press, 1982), p. 23.
2. See Jeffrie G. Murphy, "Forgiveness and Resentment," *Midwest Studies in Philosophy*, 7 (1982), pp. 503–16.
3. Ibid., p. 507.
4. Ibid., p. 505.
5. Robert C. Solomon, *The Passions* (Garden City, N.Y.: Anchor Press, 1976), p. 350.
6. Murphy, "Forgiveness and Resentment," p. 504.
7. Ibid.
8. Ibid., pp. 504–5.
9. Jeffrie G. Murphy, "Hatred: A Qualified Defense," in *Forgiveness and Mercy*, Jeffrie G. Murphy and Jean Hampton (New York: Cambridge University Press, 1988), p. 89. Although Murphy here is speaking actually of hatred, it is clear that what he says applies, pari passu, to resentment.
10. See Graham Greene, *The Tenth Man* (New York: Pocket Books, 1985).
11. 1 Samuel 18–24. This example is Murphy's. See Murphy, "Hatred," p. 89.
12. See Victor Hugo, *Les Misérables*, trans. Lee Fahnestock and Norman MacAfee (New York: New American Library, 1987), esp. pp. 1319–31.
13. Norvin Richards, "Forgiveness," *Ethics*, 99, no. 1 (October 1988), p. 82.
14. Ibid.
15. Murphy, "Hatred," p. 90.
16. Karen Horney, "The Value of Vindictiveness," *American Journal of Psychoanalysis*, 8 (1948), p. 3.
17. Murphy, "Forgiveness and Resentment," p. 505.
18. Ibid.

19. Andrew von Hirsch and Nils Jareborg, "Provocation and Culpability," in *Responsibility, Character, and the Emotions: New Essays in Moral Psychology*, ed. Ferdinand Schoeman (New York: Cambridge University Press, 1987), p. 250.

20. John Rawls, *A Theory of Justice* (Cambridge, Mass.: Harvard University Press, 1971), p. 533.

21. Michael S. Moore, "The Moral Worth of Retribution," in *Responsibility, Character, and the Emotions*, p. 211.

22. Thomas E. Hill, Jr., "Servility and Self-respect," *Monist*, 62 (January 1969), p. 97.

23. Aristotle, *Nicomachean Ethics*, trans. Terence Irwin (Indianapolis, Ind.: Hackett Publishing, 1985), v. 1126a, p. 1056.

24. Bernard Williams, "Morality and the Emotions," in *Problems of the Self* (Cambridge, England: Cambridge University Press, 1973), p. 207.

25. Aristotle, *Nicomachean Ethics*, v. 1106b25, p. 44.

26. Immanuel Kant, *The Metaphysical Principles of Virtue* (1797), trans. James Ellington (Indianapolis, Ind.: Hackett Publishing, 1983), p. 60.

27. Immanuel Kant, *Foundations of the Metaphysics of Morals* (1785), trans. Lewis White Beck (New York: Bobbs-Merrill, 1964), p. 10.

28. See O. H. Green, "Obligations regarding Passions," *Personalist*, 60 (April 1979), pp. 134–38.

29. See generally Immanuel Kant, *Fundamental Principles of the Metaphysics of Morals* (1863), trans. Thomas K. Abbott (Indianapolis, Ind.: Hackett Publishing, 1979).

30. See generally John Stuart Mill, *Utilitarianism* (1863) (Indianapolis, Ind.: Hackett Publishing, 1979).

31. See generally G. E. Moore, *Principia Ethica* (1903) (New York: Cambridge University Press, 1968).

32. See G. E. M. Anscombe, "Modern Moral Philosophy," *Philosophy*, 33 (1958), pp. 1–19.

33. See George Henrik von Wright, *The Varieties of Goodness* (London: Routledge & Kegan Paul, and New York: Humanities Press, 1963).

34. See Lawrence Becker, "The Neglect of Virtue," *Ethics*, 85 (1975), pp. 110–22.

35. See Edmund Pincoffs, "Quandary Ethics," *Mind*, 80 (1971), pp. 552–71.

36. See James Wallace, *Virtues and Vices* (Ithaca, N.Y.: Cornell University Press, 1978).

37. See Alasdair MacIntyre, *After Virtue*, 2nd ed. (Notre Dame, Ind.: University of Notre Dame Press, 1984).

38. See William Frankena, *Ethics*, 2nd ed. (Englewood Cliffs, N.J.: Prentice-Hall, 1963).

39. See Bernard Mayo, *Ethics and the Moral Life* (London: Macmillan, 1958).

40. For some of the problems that face an ethics of virtue, see Robert V. Louden, "On Some Vices of Virtue Ethics," *American Philosophical Quarterly*, 21 (July 1984), pp. 227–36.

41. See Tom Beauchamp and James Childress, *Principles of Biomedical Ethics* (New York: Oxford University Press, 1983), pp. 255–68; and Tom Beauchamp, "What's So Special about the Virtues?" in *Virtue and Medicine: Explorations in the Character of Medicine*, ed. Earl E. Shelp (Boston: D. Reidel Publishing, 1985), pp. 307–27.

42. Frankena, *Ethics*, p. 53.

43. Beauchamp, "What's So Special?" p. 310.

44. See J. Charles King, "Moral Theory and the Foundations of Social Order," in *The Libertarian Reader*, ed. Tibor R. Machan (Savage, Md.: Rowman & Littlefield, 1982), pp. 20–21.

45. See W. D. Ross, *The Nicomachean Ethics of Aristotle* (New York: Oxford University Press, 1975), pp. 28–39. See also M. F. Burnyeat, "Aristotle on Learning to Be Good," in *Essays on Aristotle's Ethics*, ed. Amelie Okesenberg Rorty (Berkeley: University of California Press, 1980), p. 69.

46. Frankena, *Ethics*, p. 53.

47. Ibid.

48. Ibid.

49. See Philippa Foot, "Virtues and Vices," in *Virtues and Vices and Other Essays in Moral Philosophy* (Berkeley: University of California Press, 1978), p. 16; emphasis added.

50. Frankena, *Ethics*, p. 53.

51. I am speaking here about the duty to *feel* benevolence. Sir David Ross, for one, believed there is a duty to act benevolently. W. D. Ross, *The Right and the Good* (Indianapolis, Ind.: Hackett Publishing, 1988), p. 21.

52. For an excellent discussion of gratitude, see Fred Berger, "Gratitude," *Ethics*, 85, no. 4 (July 1975), pp. 298–309.

53. Mill, *Utilitarianism*, p. 50.

54. Ibid.

55. Jean Hampton, "Forgiveness, Resentment, and Hatred," in *Forgiveness and Mercy*, p. 54.

56. See J. L. Mackie, "Morality and the Retributive Emotions," *Criminal Justice Ethics*, 1 (1982), pp. 3–9.

57. See Robert Axelrod, *The Evolution of Cooperation* (New York: Basic Books, 1984), chap. 8.

58. For a competing view, see Jean Hampton, "The Retributive Idea," in *Forgiveness and Mercy*, pp. 117–19.

59. Green, "Obligations," p. 136.

60. Unlike earlier, when I discussed what it means for one to express forgiveness *linguistically*, I am here employing a victim *V* to express resentment rather than a speaker *S*, since I have no stake in arguing that resentment is a performative utterance. It should be pointed out, however, that Austin

does include "resentment" on his list of behabitives. See J. L. Austin, *How to Do Things with Words*, (Cambridge, Mass.: Harvard University Press, 1962), p. 159.

61. See Immanuel Kant, *The Metaphysical Elements of Justice; Part I of the Metaphysics of Morals*, trans. John Ladd (Indianapolis, Ind.: Bobbs-Merrill, 1965), pp. 99–106.

62. See Chapter 2 and H. J. N. Horsbrugh, "Forgiveness," *Canadian Journal of Philosophy*, 4, no. 2 (December 1974), p. 279.

63. See Chapter 5, "Repentance."

64. Rawls, *Theory of Justice*, p. 533.

65. Gabriele Taylor, "Justifying the Emotions," *Mind*, 84 (July 1975), p. 396.

66. See ibid., pp. 397–98.

67. See Jane Austen, *Emma* (New York: Clarendon Press, 1925), chap. 2.

68. See Michael Moore, "Moral Worth," pp. 192 ff., for a reconstruction of Nietzsche's views on this matter.

69. Murphy, "Hatred," p. 93.

70. See David Hume, *A Treatise of Human Nature* (1739–1740), 2nd ed., ed. L. A. Selby-Bigge (New York: Oxford University Press, 1978), bk. 2, pt. 1, sec. 8.

71. "To think otherwise," says Murphy, "is to fall victim to the liberal myth of atomic individualism in its crudest form." "Hatred," p. 93. See, in this context, Rawls's discussion of the social nature of self-respect in *Theory of Justice*, pp. 440–46.

72. Bernard Boxill, "Self-respect and Protest," *Philosophy and Public Affairs*, 6 (Fall 1976), p. 67.

73. Thomas Hobbes, *Leviathan* (1651), ed. C. B. Macpherson (Harmondsworth, England, and New York: Penguin Books, 1965, 1979), chap. 10, par. 16.

74. Jean Hampton, for one, attributes this to utilitarians. See Hampton, "Forgiveness, Resentment, and Hatred," in *Forgiveness and Mercy*, p. 45. Of course, utilitarians do insist that each person counts as one.

75. See, for example, Gregory Pence, "Recent Work on Virtues," *American Philosophical Quarterly*, 21, no. 4 (October 1984), pp. 281–97.

76. See Foot, "Virtues and Vices," pp. 1–18.

77. More precisely, Tolstoy has Prince Andre declare, "If every one would only fight for his own convictions, there'd be no war." See Leo Tolstoy, *War and Peace*, trans. Constance Garnett (New York: Modern Library, n.d.), p. 19. Of course, we could also argue that there would be no war if everyone was servile.

78. Foot, "Virtues and Vices," p. 5.

79. Elizabeth Beardsley, "Understanding and Forgiveness," in *The Philosophy of Brand Blanshard*, ed. Paul A. Schlipp (LaSalle, Ill.: Open Court, 1981), p. 255.

80. See Aristotle, *Nicomachean Ethics*, v. 1125b, p. 105. *Epiekia* means "reasonable" when applied to persons and "equitable" when applied to "actions." I thank Jacob Stern for bringing this to my attention.

5 The Ethics of Forgiveness

1. Jeffrie G. Murphy, "Hatred: A Qualified Defense," in *Forgiveness and Mercy*, Jeffrie G. Murphy and Jean Hampton (New York: Cambridge University Press, 1988), p. 89.
2. See Jeffrie G. Murphy, "Forgiveness and Resentment," in *Forgiveness and Mercy*, p. 24.
3. In this context, consider S. J. Perelman's remark: "To err is human; to forgive, supine."
4. Literally, *metanoia* is a religious term originating in the Old Testament, meaning "conversion to God." More generally, it means "change of heart."
5. This idea is suggested by Jeffrie Murphy. See his "Forgiveness and Resentment," *Midwest Studies in Philosophy*, 7 (1982), pp. 503–16 (not to be confused with his book chapter going by the same title; see note 2 above). For the distinction between Murphy's position and mine, see the penultimate section of this chapter.
6. See Martin Golding, "Forgiveness and Regret," *Philosophical Forum*, 16, nos. 1–2 (Winter/Fall 1984–1985), pp. 121–37.
7. Ibid., pp. 126–30.
8. Ibid., p. 126.
9. Ibid.
10. Ibid., p. 127.
11. Ibid., p. 128.
12. Ibid., p. 129.
13. I might add to this that, in the absence of a promise of a personal nature, forgiveness is impossible, since the victim is ignorant of the wrongdoer's identity.
14. See Max Scheler, *On the Eternal in Man*, trans. Bernard Nobel (New York: Harper & Brothers, 1960), pp. 38–39.
15. Benedict de Spinoza, *Short Treatise on God, Man and His Well-being*, trans. A. Wolf (New York: Russell and Russell, 1967), bk. 2, chap. 10.
16. William James, *The Varieties of Religious Experience* (New York: Mentor Books, 1958), p. 116.
17. Murphy, "Forgiveness and Resentment," *Midwest Studies*, p. 504.
18. See Kant, *Religion within the Limits of Reason Alone* (1792), trans. Theodore M. Greene and Hoyt H. Hudson (New York: Harper & Row, 1960), pp. 64–65.
19. Ibid.
20. John Silber, "The Ethical Significance of Kant's *Religion*," foreword to ibid., p. cxxxiii.

Against Silber's interpretation, Allan Wood has argued that forgiveness *is* consistent with Kant's moral philosophy. As Wood sees it, throughout the *Religion*, Kant maintains that the person of good disposition may put her faith in God's grace and that God's grace is something *rational*. Thus, according to Wood, Kant would differ from someone like Kierkegaard, who regards our faith in God's forgiveness as irrational and an offense to reason. See Søren Kierkegaard, *Fear and Trembling*, trans. Walter Lowrie (Garden City, N.Y.: Doubleday, 1954), p. 80; see also *The Sickness unto Death*, trans. Walter Lowrie (Garden City, N.Y.: Doubleday, 1954), pp. 244ff.; and *Repetition: An Essay in Experimental Psychology*, trans. Walter Lowrie (New York: Harper & Row, 1964), pp. 132ff.

Nor, according to Wood, could Kant accept the sentimentalism of a Feuerbach, who writes,

> Only the love which has flesh and blood can absolve from the sins which flesh and blood commit. A merely mortal being cannot forgive what is contrary to the law of morality. . . . The moral judge, who does not infuse human blood into his judgment, judges the sinner relentlessly, inexorably. . . . The negation or annulling of sin is the negation of abstract moral rectitude—the positing of love, mercy, sensibility.

Ludwig Feuerbach, *The Essence of Christianity*, trans. Georg Eliot (Harper & Row, 1957), 60g, 48fe.

According to Wood, Kant does not reject the humane sentiments of Feuerbach. He regards a forgiving disposition as a morally good quality and holds that a conciliatory spirit is a duty of virtue. What Kant does reject is a view of forgiveness which lacks a rational foundation, because such a view is unable to distinguish forgiveness from simple immorality. Only a forgiveness that is compatible with the moral law can command respect. See Allan W. Wood, *Kant's Moral Religion* (Ithaca, N.Y.: Cornell University Press, 1970), pp. 239–43.

21. Kant, *Religion*, pp. 64–65.

22. See Norvin Richards, "Forgiveness," *Ethics*, 99, no. 1 (October 1988), pp. 77–97.

23. Ibid., p. 88.

24. Ibid.

25. Susan Jacoby, *Wild Justice: The Evolution of Revenge* (New York: Harper & Row, 1983), p. 347.

26. Ibid.

27. Technically speaking, X only represents that she respects the rule of morality that she had violated in the act that led to V's particular injury.

28. See "Expressing Resentment" in Chapter 4.

29. See John L. Austin, *How to Do Things with Words*, (Cambridge, Mass.: Harvard University Press, 1962), p. 159.

30. See Aurel Kolnai, "Forgiveness," in *Ethics, Value, and Reality: Se-*

lected Papers of Aurel Kolnai*, eds. Bernard Williams and David Wiggins (Indianapolis, Ind.: Hackett Publishing, 1978), pp. 215–17.

31. P. Twambley, "Mercy and Forgiveness," *Analysis*, 36 (January 1976), p. 90. See note 4 above.

32. Herbert Fingarette, "Guilt," *American Philosophical Quarterly* (1979), reprinted in *Virtues and Values: An Introduction to Ethics*, ed. Joshua Halberstam (Englewood Cliffs, N.J.: Prentice-Hall, 1988), p. 179.

33. Anthony Trollope, *Orley Farm* (Oxford, England: Oxford University Press, 1950), p. 63, cited in Stanley Hauerwas, "Constancy and Forgiveness: The Novel as a School for Virtue," *Notre Dame English Journal*, 15 (1983), p. 35; emphasis added.

34. Murphy, "Forgiveness and Resentment," in *Forgiveness and Resentment*, p. 29.

35. See Immanuel Kant, *Fundamental Principles of the Metaphysics of Morals* (1785), trans. Thomas K. Abbott (Indianapolis, Ind.: Bobbs-Merrill, 1949), pp. 38–39. For the distinction between perfect and imperfect duties, see Bruce Aune, *Kant's Theory of Morals* (Princeton, N.J.: Princeton University Press, 1979), pp. 188–94. See also Onora Nell, *Acting on Principle: An Essay on Kantian Ethics* (New York: Columbia University Press, 1975), pp. 48ff.

36. Murphy, "Forgiveness and Mercy," in *Forgiveness and Mercy*, p. 29.

37. John Rawls, *A Theory of Justice* (Cambridge, Mass.: Harvard University Press, 1971), p. 534.

38. Hannah Arendt, "Irreversibility and the Power to Forgive," in *The Human Condition* (Chicago: University of Chicago Press, 1958), p. 237.

39. See Shulcan Aruch, 606. For a discussion of forgiveness in Jewish theology, see Louis E. Newman's "The Quality of Mercy: On the Duty to Forgive in the Judaic Tradition," *Journal of Religious Ethics*, 15 (Fall 1987), pp. 155–72. Also of interest is Joseph Soloveitchik's *On Repentance: The Thoughts and Oral Discourses of Rabbi Joseph B. Soloveitchik*, ed. Pinchas H. Peli (New York: Paulist Press, 1984), pp. 270–73.

40. Murphy, "Forgiveness and Mercy," in *Forgiveness and Mercy*, p. 24.

41. Ibid.

42. Ibid.

43. Ibid., p. 26.

44. Ibid.

45. Ibid.

46. Jean Hampton, "Forgiveness, Resentment, and Hatred," in *Forgiveness and Mercy*, p. 84n.

47. Murphy, "Forgiveness and Mercy," in *Forgiveness and Mercy*, pp. 26–27.

48. This point is also made by Hampton, "Forgiveness, Resentment, and Hatred," p. 84n.

49. Murphy, "Forgiveness and Mercy," in *Forgiveness and Mercy*, p. 29.

50. Richards, "Forgiveness," p. 92.

51. Thomas E. Hill, Jr., "Servility and Self-respect," *Monist*, 62 (January 1969), p. 97.

52. Richard Fitzgibbons, "The Cognitive and Emotive Uses of Forgiveness in the Treatment of Anger," *Psychotherapy*, 23, no. 4 (Winter 1986), p. 630.

53. I owe this observation to Steven Ross.

54. See especially Chapter 2, "The Presuppositions of Forgiveness."

55. Murphy, "Forgiveness and Mercy," in *Forgiveness and Mercy*, p. 20.

56. Matthew 18:21–35.

57. Murphy, "Forgiveness and Mercy," in *Forgiveness and Mercy*, p. 32.

58. René Descartes, *Meditations on First Philosophy*, trans. Donald A. Cress (Indianapolis, Ind.: Hackett Publishing, 1979), meditation 1, p. 13.

59. Sissela Bok, *Lying* (New York: Pantheon Books, 1978), p. 31n. For an excellent discussion of trust, see Annette Baier, "Trust and Antitrust," *Ethics*, 96, no. 2 (January 1986), pp. 231–61.

Bibliography

Adams, Marilyn. "God and Forgiveness." *Faith and Philosophy*, 8, no. 3 (July 1991).

Alston, William P. "Moral Attitudes and Moral Judgments." *Nous*, 2 (1968), 1–23.

———. *Philosophy of Language*. Englewood Cliffs, N.J.: Prentice-Hall, 1964.

Anscombe, G. E. M. "Modern Moral Philosophy." *Philosophy*, 33 (1958), 1–19.

Aquinas, Thomas. *Summa Theologica* (1265–1273). Volumes 4–12 of the Leonine edition. Rome, 1918–1930. Also as *The Summa Theologica*. Translated by the English Dominican Fathers. 22 Volumes. London, 1912–1936. Appears in *Basic Writings of Saint Thomas Aquinas*. Edited by A. C. Pegis. New York: Benziger, 1947.

———. *Summa de Veritate Catholicae Didei contra Gentiles* (1259–1264). Volumes 13–15 of the Leonine edition. Rome, 1918–1930. Also published in a one-volume "manual" edition. Turin and Rome, 1934. Also as *St. Thomas Aquinas: On the Truth of the Catholic Faith*. Translated by A. C. Pegis, J. F. Anderson, V. J. Bourke, and C. J. O'Neill. 5 Volumes. New York: Doubleday, 1955.

Arendt, Hannah. "Irreversibility and the Power to Forgive." In *The Human Condition*. Chicago: University of Illinois Press, 1958.

Aristotle. *Nicomachean Ethics*. Translated by Terence Irwin. Indianapolis, Ind.: Hackett Publishing, 1985.

Aune, Bruce. *Kant's Theory of Morals*. Princeton, N.J.: Princeton University Press, 1979.

Austen, Jane. *Emma*. New York: Clarendon Press, 1925.

Austin, John Langshaw. *How to Do Things with Words*. Cambridge, Mass.: Harvard University Press, 1962.

———. "Performative-Constative." In *The Philosophy of Language*. Edited by J. R. Searle. Oxford, England: Oxford University Press, 1977.

———. "Performative Utterances." In *Philosophical Papers*. New York: Oxford University Press, 1970.

———. "A Plea for Excuses." *Proceedings of the Aristotelian Society*, 57 (1956–1957), 1–30.

Axelrod, Robert. *The Evolution of Cooperation*. New York: Basic Books, 1984.

Baier, Annette. "Trust and Antitrust." *Ethics*, 96 (1986), 231–61.

Baier, Kurt. "The Meaning of Life." In *Philosophy: The Basic Issues*. 2nd Edition. Edited by E. Klemke, David Kline, and Robert Hollinger. New York: St. Martin's Press, 1986.

Beardsley, Elizabeth. "Moral Disapproval and Moral Indignation." *Philosophy and Phenomenological Research*, 31 (1970), 161–76.

———. "Moral Worth and Moral Credit." *Philosophical Review*, 66 (1957), 304–28.

———. "Understanding and Forgiveness." In *The Philosophy of Brand Blanshard*. Edited by Paul Schlipp. LaSalle, Ill.: Open Court, 1980.

Beatty, Joseph. "Forgiveness." *American Philosophical Quarterly*, 7 (1970), 246–52.

Beauchamp, Tom. "The Justification of Moral Beliefs." In *Philosophical Ethics: An Introduction to Moral Philosophy*. New York: McGraw-Hill, 1982.

———. "What's So Special about the Virtues?" In *Virtue and Medicine: Explorations in the Character of Medicine*. Edited by Earl Shelp. Boston: D. Reidel Publishing, 1985.

Beauchamp, Tom, and James Childress. *Principles of Biomedical Ethics*. New York: Oxford University Press, 1983.

Beccaria, Cesare. "Pardons." In *On Crimes and Punishments*. Translated by David Young. Indianapolis, Ind.: Hackett Publishing, 1986. First published in 1764.

Becker, Lawrence. "The Neglect of Virtue." *Ethics*, 85 (1975), 110–22.

Berger, Fred. "Gratitude." *Ethics*, 85, no. 4 (July 1975), 298–309.

Berlin, Isaiah. "Two Concepts of Liberty." In *Four Essays on Liberty*. New York: Oxford University Press, 1979.

Bishop, Sharon. "Connections and Guilt." *Hypatia*, 2 (1987), 7–23.

Blanshard, Brand. "Reply to Elizabeth L. Beardsley." In *The Philosophy of Brand Blanshard*. Edited by Paul Schlipp. LaSalle, Ill.: Open Court, 1980.

———. "Retribution Revisited." In *Philosophical Perspectives on Punish-*

ment. Edited by E. Ḥ. Medon, et al. Springfield, Ill.: Charles C. Thomas, 1968.

Bok, Sissela. *Lying: Moral Choice in Public and Private Life*. New York: Pantheon Books, 1978.

Boxhill, Bernard. "Self-respect and Protest." *Philosophy and Public Affairs*, 6 (Fall 1976), 58–69.

Bradley, F. H. *Ethical Studies*. Oxford, England: Oxford University Press, 1927.

Brandt, R. B. "A Moral Principle about Killing." In *Intervention and Reflection: Basic Issues in Medical Ethics*. 2nd Edition. Edited by Ronald Munson. Belmont, Calif.: Wadsworth Publishing, 1983.

Bristle, Bob, and Carol McGinnis. *When It's Hard to Forgive*. Wheaton, Ill.: Victor Books, 1982.

Burnyeat, M. F. "Aristotle on Learning to Be Good." In *Essays on Aristotelian Ethics*. Edited by Amelie Okesenberg Rorty. Berkeley: University of California Press, 1980.

Butler, Joseph. *Fifteen Sermons*. London: The English Theological Libruary, 1726.

Card, Claudia. "Mercy." *Philosophical Review*, 81 (1972), 182–207.

Coke, Sir Edward. *The Third Part of the Institutes of the Laws of England*. 1817.

Danto, Arthur. *Nietzsche as Philosopher*. New York: Macmillan, 1965.

Descartes, René. *Meditations on First Philosophy*. Translated by Donald A. Cress. Indianapolis, Ind.: Hackett Publishing, 1979. First published in 1641.

Dostoyevsky, Fyodor. *The Brothers Karamazov*. Translated by Constance Garnett. New York: Signet Classics, 1980.

———. *The Idiot*. Translated by Constance Garnett. New York: Signet Classics, 1987. First published in 1868.

Downie, R. S. "Forgiveness." *Philosophical Quarterly*, 15 (1965), 128–34.

Dummett, Michael. "Truth." *Proceedings of the Aristotelian Society*, 59 (1958–1959), 141–62.

Ewing, A. C. *The Morality of Punishment*. Montclair, N.J.: Patterson-Smith, 1970.

Feinberg, Joel. "Action and Responsibility." In *Doing and Deserving: Essays in the Theory of Responsibility*. Princeton, N.J.: Princeton University Press, 1970.

———. "The Expressive Function of Punishment." In *Doing and Deserving: Essays in the Theory of Responsibility*. Princeton, N.J.: Princeton University Press, 1970.

———. "Justice and Personal Desert." In *Doing and Deserving: Essays in the Theory of Responsibility*. Princeton, N.J.: Princeton University Press, 1970.

Feuerbach, Ludwig. *The Essence of Christianity*. Translated by Georg Eliot. New York: Harper & Row, 1957.

Fingarette, Herbert. "Guilt." *American Philosophical Quarterly* (1979). Reprinted in *Virtues and Values: An Introduction to Ethics*. Edited by Joshua Halberstam. Englewood Cliffs, N.J.: Prentice-Hall, 1988.

Fitzgibbons, Richard. "The Cognitive and Emotive Uses of Forgiveness in the Treatment of Anger." *Psychotherapy*, 23 (1986), 629–32.

Flew, Anthony. "The Justification of Punishment." *Philosophy*, 29 (1954).

Foot, Philippa. "Virtues and Vices." In *Virtues and Vices and Other Essays in Moral Philosophy*. Berkeley: University of California Press, 1978.

Frankena, William. *Ethics*. 2nd Edition. Englewood Cliffs, N.J.: Prentice-Hall, 1973.

Freeman, James. "Affective Rationality." Unpublished paper, 1983.

Geach, Peter. *The Virtues*. Cambridge, England: Cambridge University Press, 1977.

Gingell, John. "Forgiveness and Power." *Analysis*, 34 (1974), 180–83.

Golding, Martin. "Forgiveness and Regret." *Philosophical Forum*, 16 (1984–1985), 121–37.

Green, O. H. "Obligations Regarding Passions." *Personalist*, 60 (1979), 134–38.

Greene, Graham. *The Tenth Man*. New York: Pocket Books, 1985.

Hampton, Jean. "Forgiveness, Resentment, and Hatred." In *Forgiveness and Mercy*, Jeffrie G. Murphy and Jean Hampton. New York: Cambridge University Press, 1988.

———. "The Retributive Idea." In *Forgiveness and Mercy*, Jeffrie G. Murphy and Jean Hampton. New York: Cambridge University Press, 1988.

Hauerwas, Stanley. "Constancy and Forgiveness: The Novel as a School for Virtue." *Notre Dame English Journal*, 15 (1983), 23–54.

Hegel, G. W. F. *Philosophy of Right*. Translated by T. M. Knox. Oxford, England: Oxford University Press, 1942.

Held, Virginia. *Rights and Goods: Justifying Social Action*. New York: Free Press, 1984.

Hill, Thomas E., Jr., "Servility and Self-respect." *Monist*, 62 (1969), 87–104.

Hobbes, Thomas. *Leviathan*. Edited by C. B. MacPherson. Harmondsworth, England, and New York: Penguin Books, 1979. First published in 1651.

Holborow, L. C. "Praise, Blame, and Credit." *Proceedings of the Aristotelian Society*, 72 (1971–1972).

Horney, Karen. "The Value of Vindictiveness." *American Journal of Psychoanalysis*, 8 (1948), 3–12.

Horsbrugh, H. J. N. "Forgiveness." *Canadian Journal of Philosophy*, 4 (1974), 269–82.

Hughes, Martin. "Forgiveness." *Analysis*, 35 (1975), 113–17.

Hugo, Victor. *Les Misérables*. Translated by Lee Fahestock and Norman MacAfee. New York: New American Library, 1987. First published in 1862.

Hume, David. *A Treatise of Human Nature* (1739–1740). 2nd Edition. Edited by L. A. Selby-Bigge. New York: Oxford University Press, 1978. First published in 1888.

Jacoby, Susan. *Wild Justice: The Evolution of Revenge*. New York: Harper & Row, 1983.

James, William. *The Varieties of Religious Experience*. New York: Mentor Books, 1958.

Kant, Immanuel. *Foundations of the Metaphysics of Morals*. Translated by Lewis White Beck. New York: Bobbs-Merrill, 1964. First published in 1785.

———. *The Metaphysical Elements of Justice*. Translated by John Ladd. Indianapolis, Ind.: Bobbs-Merrill, 1965. First published in 1797.

———. *The Metaphysical Principles of Virtue*. Translated by James Ellington. Indianapolis, Ind.: Hackett Publishing, 1983. First published in 1797.

———. *Religion within the Limits of Reason Alone*. Translated by Theodore M. Greene and Hoyt H. Hudson. New York: Harper & Row, 1960. First published in 1792.

Kavka, Gregory S. "Wrongdoing and Guilt." *Journal of Philosophy*, 71 (1974), 663–64.

Kenny, Anthony. *Wittgenstein*. Cambridge, Mass.: Harvard University Press, 1974.

Kierkegaard, Søren. *Fear and Trembling*. Translated by Walter Lowrie. Garden City, N.Y.: Doubleday, 1954.

———. *Repetition: An Essay in Experimental Psychology*. Translated by Walter Lowrie. New York: Harper & Row, 1964.

———. *The Sickness unto Death*. Translated by Walter Lowrie. Garden City, N.Y.: Doubleday, 1954.

King, J. Charles. "Moral Theory and the Foundations of Social Order." In *The Libertarian Reader*. Edited by Tibor R. Machan. Savage, Md.: Rowman and Littlefield, 1982.

Kolnai, Aurel. "Forgiveness." *Proceedings of the Aristotelian Society*, 74 (1973–1974), 91–106. Reprinted in *Ethics, Value, and Reality: Selected Papers of Aurel Kolnai*. Edited by Bernard Williams and David Wiggins. Indianapolis, Ind.: Hackett Publishing, 1978.

Lewis, Meirlys. "On Forgiveness." *Philosophical Quarterly*, 30 (1980), 235–45.

Louden, Robert B. "On Some Vices of Virtue Ethics." *American Philosophical Quarterly*, 21 (1984), 227–36.

Lyons, William. *Emotions*. Cambridge, England: Cambridge University Press, 1980.

Mabbott, J. D. "Punishment." *Mind*, 48 (1939), 41–57.

MacIntyre, Alasdair. *After Virtue*. 2nd Edition. Notre Dame, Ind.: University of Notre Dame Press, 1984.

Mackie, J. L. "Morality and the Retributive Emotions." *Criminal Justice Ethics*, 1 (1982), 3–10.

Mayo, Bernard. *Ethics and the Moral Life*. London: Macmillan, 1958.

Mill, John Stuart. "Remarks on Bentham's Philosophy." Volume 10 of *Collected Works*. Edited by J. M. Robson. Toronto, Canada: University of Toronto Press, 1968.

———. *Utilitarianism*. Indianapolis, Ind.: Hackett Publishing, 1979. First published in 1863.

Minas, Anne. "God and Forgiveness." *Philosophical Quarterly*, 25 (1975), 138–50.

Moore, G. E. *Principia Ethica*. New York: Cambridge University Press, 1968. First published in 1903.

Moore, Kathleen Dean. *Pardons: Justice, Mercy, and the Public Interest*. New York: Oxford University Press, 1989.

Moore, Michael. "The Moral Worth of Retribution." *Responsibility, Character, and the Emotions: New Essays in Moral Psychology*. Edited by Ferdinand Schoeman. New York: Cambridge University Press, 1987.

Morris, Herbert. "Murphy on Forgiveness." *Criminal Justice Ethics*, 7, no. 2 (1988), 15–19.

———. "Persons and Punishment." *Monist*, 52 (1968), 475–501.

Murphy, Jeffrie G. "Forgiveness and Resentment." *Midwest Studies in Philosophy*, 7 (1982), 503–16.

———. "Forgiveness and Resentment." In *Forgiveness and Mercy*, Jeffrie G. Murphy and Jean Hampton. New York: Cambridge University Press, 1988.

———. "Hatred: A Qualified Defense." In *Forgiveness and Mercy*, Jeffrie G. Murphy and Jean Hampton. New York: Cambridge University Press, 1988.

———. "Mercy and Legal Justice." In *Forgiveness and Mercy*, Jeffrie G. Murphy and Jean Hampton. New York: Cambridge University Press, 1988.

Narayan, Uma. "Varieties of Forgiveness." Lecture presented at the American Philosophical Association, Eastern Division, 86th Annual Meeting. Atlanta, 1989.

Neblett, William. "Forgiveness and Ideals." *Mind*, 83 (1974).

Nell, Onora. *Acting on Principle: An Essay on Kantian Ethics*. New York: Columbia University Press, 1975.

Newman, Louis E. "The Quality of Mercy: On the Duty to Forgive in the Judaic Tradition." *Journal of Religious Studies*, 15 (Fall 1987), 155–72.

Nietzsche, Friedrich. *Beyond Good and Evil*. Translated by Walter Kaufmann. New York: Vintage Books, 1966.

———. *On the Genealogy of Morals and Ecce Homo*. Translated by Walter Kaufmann. New York: Vintage Books, 1969.

North, Joanna. "Wrongdoing and Forgiveness." *Philosophy*, 62 (1987), 499–508.

O'Shaughnessy, R. J., "Forgiveness." *Philosophy*, 42 (1967), 336–52.

Pascal, Blaise. *Pensées*. Translated by A. J. Krailsheimer. New York: Penguin Classics, 1984. First published in 1662.

Pence, Gregory. "Recent Works on Virtues." *American Philosophical Quarterly*, 21, no. 4 (October 1984), 281–97.

Phillips, Derek. "Authenticiteit or Moraliteit?" *Wijsgerig Perspectief op Maatschappij en Wetenschap*, 22 (1982). Reprinted as "Authenticity or Morality?" In *The Virtues: Contemporary Essays on Moral Character*. Edited by Robert B. Kruschwitz and Robert C. Roberts. Belmont, Calif.: Wadsworth Publishing, 1987.

Pincoffs, Edmund. "Quandary Ethics." *Mind*, 80 (1971), 552–72.

Plutarch. "On the Control of Anger." *Moralia*. Volume 6. London: Heinemann, 1958.

Rashdall, Hastings. "The Ethics of Forgiveness." *Ethics*, 10 (1900), 193–206.

Rawls, John. *A Theory of Justice*. Cambridge, Mass.: Harvard University Press, 1971.

Richards, Norvin. "Forgiveness." *Ethics*, 99 (1988), 77–97.

Ross, W. D. *The Nicomachean Ethics of Aristotle*. New York: Oxford University Press, 1975.

———. *The Right and the Good*. Indianapolis, Ind.: Hackett Publishing, 1988. First published in 1930.

Sartre, Jean-Paul. *Anti-Semite and Jew*. Translated by George J. Becker. New York: Schocken Books, 1948.

———. *Being and Nothingness*. Translated by Hazel Barnes. New York: Philosophical Library, 1956.

Scheler, Max. *On the Eternal in Man.* Translated by Bernard Nobel. New York: Harper & Brothers, 1960.

———. *Ressentiment.* Translated by Holdheim. New York: Free Press, 1961.

Searle, J. R. "Introduction." In *The Philosophy of Language.* Edited by J. R. Searle. Oxford, England: Oxford University Press, 1977.

Seneca, Lucius. "On Anger." In *Moral Essays.* Volume 2. Cambridge, Mass.: Harvard University Press, 1958.

Shakespeare, William. "The Tempest." In *The Plays of Shakespeare.* Edited by Sandy Lesberg. New York: Peebles Classic Library, n.d.

Sidgwick, Henry. *The Methods of Ethics.* 7th Edition. London: Macmillan, 1963. First published in 1874.

Silber, John. "The Ethical Significance of Kant's *Religion.*" Foreword to *Religion within the Limits of Reason Alone,* Immanuel Kant. New York: Harper & Row, 1960.

Smart, Alwynne. "Mercy." *Philosophy,* 43 (October 1968), 345–59.

Solomon, Robert C. *The Passions.* Garden City, N.Y.: Anchor Press, 1976.

Soloveitchik, Joseph. *On Repentance.* Translated by Pinchas H. Peli. New York: Paulist Press, 1984.

Sommers, Christina Hoff, Editor. *Vice and Virtue in Everyday Life: Introductory Readings in Ethics.* New York: Harcourt, Brace, Jovanovich, 1985.

Spinoza, Benedict de. *Short Treatise on God, Man and His Well-being.* Translated by A. Wolf. New York: Russell and Russell, 1967.

Steere, Douglas V., Editor. *Spiritual Counsels and Letters of Baron von Hugel.* London: Darton, Longman, and Todd, 1959.

Strawson, P.F. "Freedom and Resentment." *Proceedings of the British Academy,* 48 (1962). Reprinted in *Freedom and Resentment and Other Essays.* Edited by P. F. Strawson. Oxford, England: Methuen, 1974.

Taylor, Gabriele. "Justifying the Emotions." *Mind,* 84 (1975), 390–402.

Theroux, Alexander. "Revenge." *Harper's Magazine* (1982).

Tolstoy, Leo. *Resurrection.* Translated by Rosemary Edmunds. New York: Penguin Books, 1983.

———. *War and Peace.* Translated by Constance Garnett. New York: Modern Library, n.d.

Trollope, Anthony. *Orley Farm.* Oxford, England: Oxford University Press, 1950.

Twambley, P. "Mercy and Forgiveness." *Analysis,* 36 (1976), 84–90.

Urmson, J. O. "John Langshaw Austin." In *Encyclopedia of Philosophy.* New York: Macmillan, 1967.

———. "Saints and Heroes." *Essays in Moral Philosophy*. Edited by A. I. Melden. Seattle: University of Washington Press, 1958.

Von Hirsch, Andrew and Nils Jareborg. "Provocation and Culpability." In *Responsibility, Character, and the Emotions: New Essays in Moral Psychology*. Edited by Ferdinand Schoeman. New York: Cambridge University Press, 1987.

Von Wright, Georg Henrik. *The Varieties of Goodness*. London: Routledge & Kegan Paul, and New York: Humanities Press, 1963.

Wallace, James. *Virtues and Vices*. Ithaca, N.Y.: Cornell University Press, 1978.

Wiesenthal, Simon. *The Sunflower*. London: W. H. Allen, 1972.

Williams, Bernard. "Deciding to Believe." In *Problems of the Self*. Cambridge, England: Cambridge University Press, 1973.

———. "Morality and the Emotions." In *Problems of the Self*. Cambridge, England: Cambridge University Press, 1973.

Wood, Allan W. *Kant's Moral Religion*. Ithaca, N.Y.: Cornell University Press, 1970.

Index

About the Author

JORAM GRAF HABER (b. 1955) teaches philosophy at Bergen Community College in Paramus, New Jersey. He received his Ph.D. from the Graduate School of the City University of New York and has a J.D. from Pace University School of Law. He has published a number of articles in applied ethics and is the author of *Doing and Being: Selected Readings in Moral Philosophy* (Macmillan, 1993), the editor of *Absolutism and Its Consequentialist Critics* (Rowman & Littlefield, 1993), and the co-editor, with Steven M. Cahn, of *Twentieth-Century Ethical Theory* (to be published by Macmillan in 1994).